Escaping the Grip of Narcissism

A Guide to Identifying and Healing from Toxic Relationships

Monday Farouq

Escaping the Grip of Narcissism: A Guide to Identifying and Healing from Toxic Relationships

Copyright © 2024 by **Monday Farouq**

Table of content

Introduction: Recognizing the Toll of Narcissistic Abuse

The scars caused by narcissistic abuse are deeper than you may imagine them to be. The odds are that you may have felt the pain the narcissist brings into your life—a friend, a romantic partner, a family member, or even a work colleague. The emotional turbulence, the inner absence, the destruction of your self-esteem—it's a pain that can make you feel lost, blurred, and completely exhausted.

What you should know from the start is that none of this is your fault. The self-centered, manipulative, and cruel behavior of the narcissist is a reflection of their deep insecurity and lack of empathy, not a reflection on you. Nevertheless, the fact of narcissistic abuse is that it can make you doubt everything in you, from the contents of your perception of reality to your core self-identity.

When you embark on your journey to recovery, you need to recognize the broad impact that narcissistic abuse has had on your total welfare. The unbreakable links, the self-doubt, the haunting remnants of shame and incompetence—all are common experiences for the victim of a narcissistic relationship. You must value yourself, and the hurt is something you need not just move on from.

Narcissistic abuse is a sophisticated and subcutaneous form of emotional manipulation that often leads to deep scars on the mind. It goes beyond the capacity to just get over and move on with our lives. The moral sense, the endless craving for validation, the changing goalposts—these are all tactics aimed at breaking down your self-esteem, your boundaries, and your ability to rely on your intuition.

Quite probably, you would have found yourself asking those inner questions like whether you are "too sensitive" or "being overreactive," or whether you have been constantly reviled and treated as if your worth is nothing. The belittling of you by the narcissist where you're made to feel irrelevant, insignificant, and unworthy is one of the intellectualities of their abuse.

Besides the mental and emotional toll, there is also the physical and financial toll that narcissistic abuse can incur. The narcissist may use blatant physical violence as a means to assert dominance or may adopt more covert avenues to manipulate and control you, leaving you feeling trapped and vulnerable. Financial abuse and the destruction of your work and study life are all methods the narcissist uses to maintain control over you.

Yet the most cunning component is that it subtly messes with your self-confidence. Token after token, the trivialization, the uncertainty, and disregard for your feelings and wants— they all damage your capability of trusting your sensations and emotions. There's a chance you might start overthinking all your choices and interactions, doubting yourself, wondering if you're "exaggerating" or "overdoing things."

This is the real sadness of narcissistic abuse: the way it can strip you of your self-worth, your personal space, and your capacity to confidently navigate the world with clarity. It is a drama that can make you believe that you are a stranger and there is no one around from whom you can get help.

But do not worry, my dear, because you are not alone. Tons of people walk this way before you. They all end up tougher, stronger, and smarter for it. This book is proof of the healing power, the invincible human spirit, and the will of one to find self-awareness once again in the harshest circumstances.

As you read this book, and the pages turn, know that this journey is one of self-discovery, of re-grasping the power that was taken away from you, and of creating a life that is truly and authentically yours. It will be a long journey, but with appropriate tools, a supportive environment, and unstoppable determination to heal, you can leave those shadows of narcissistic abuse and come out as whole and empowered.

Therefore, take a deep breath, and let's just start working on reestablishing yourself. The road ahead may be circuitous and hard to walk through, but you'll be drawing closer and closer to the ultimate liberation and fulfillment you dream of.

Part I: Understanding the Narcissistic Personality

As we start this -journey of regaining our authentic selves, we must start by exploring the complex and typically misconceived world of narcissism. Although the use of the word "narcissist" has become almost a buzzword in modern lives, it is important to keep in mind that narcissistic personality disorder is a deeply rooted and multi-faceted issue that can wreak havoc in the lives of victims and loved ones.

The narcissist and their capacity to affect our lives can only be grasped if we first remove the layers of their self-serving mask. Beneath the pretense of charisma, charm, and excessive self-importance is a vulnerable and insecure individual with a non-stop need for admiration, validation, and control.

What is at the center of the narcissistic personality is an overwhelming feeling of superiority and a serious absence of empathy. Narcissists do not communicate with people they like and love but with those who recognize their thoughts of being the best in the room.

The result is narcissists developing distorted worldviews and engaging in a variety of manipulative and exploitative behaviors including gaslighting and emotional abuse to financial and physical control. They are true masters of deception, being able to easily hide the real intentions behind the false mask of charm and charisma.

However, don't be deceived – behind this mask lies a chip off a block ego, one that needs to be always propped up and validated. Narcissists not only are oversensitive to any hint of insult or criticism, but they will do whatever they can to preserve their illusion of self-superiority, even at the expense of those who are close to them.

When considering the defining features of the narcissistic personality, we should keep in mind that narcissism is situational. Not all people, who demonstrate some narcissistic traits, will satisfy the criteria of a full-blown Narcissistic Personality Disorder (NPD). Nevertheless, knowing the mechanisms that push narcissistic behavior can be a very useful tool for recognizing and managing the toxic dynamics that can occur within our relationships.

Maybe you have a hardcore narcissist in your life or just an occasional "narcissistic flare," but in the next part, we'll equip you with the necessity knowledge and awareness you need to protect yourself and your self-esteem.

And now, let's go deeper into the psyche of narcissism, unraveling the intricacies of this complex and often misjudged disorder. Be mindful that the purpose of this is not to demonize or psychopathologize the narcissist but to equip you with practical tools to help you overcome the narcissist's toxic influence and concentrate on rebuilding your life.

Chapter 1: Defining Narcissism: The Hallmarks of a Narcissistic Mindset

Introduction to Narcissistic Personality Disorder (NPD)

This journey starts with us gaining a profound insight into the narcissistic personality, the mechanisms, and the dynamics that drive and embed the disorder to show us how deep the problem runs. Narcissistic Personality Disorder (NPD) is an intricate and multifold construct that presents a host of dysfunctional behaviors and perceptions arising from a self-distortion sense and a continual aspiration for authority, control, and recognition.

At the core of NPD lies a narcissistic belief system, which is comprised of a grandiose self, following which the narcissist values him/herself as better and superior, entitled and deserving. Also, this narcissistic philosophy demands the narcissist of those around to admire him/her. It is narcissists themselves who use this facade. They believe that if they affect others a certain way, others will treat them in the same manner and they will not find out that the narcissist's insecurity, emptiness, and fear of rejection are just hidden inside.

A narcissist's desire to constantly maintain a highly inflated self-image is contingent on the building blocks of empathy, compassion, and concern for others which unfortunately often comes at these others' expense. As a trait of narcissistic personality disorder, people who have this disorder typically don't respect other people's thoughts, feelings, health, and well-being and exploit those whom they live with, using all those people for their selfish agenda. With this insensitivity to fellow human beings, narcissists harden their hearts and bones. They are callous and thus, their victims have to undergo a humongous amount of grief and agony.

As we dig into NPD complexity, it becomes clear that this disorder can be classified on a spectrum, resulting in different levels of seriousness and complexity. On one hand, the manifestation of narcissism tends to be more grandiose and outwardly expressed by some individuals, and for others, it may transpire in a covert manner where they hide their feelings of entitlement and superiority under the guise of fragility and victimhood. However, narcissism can show up in different ways, although the common factor is the twisted perception of self, the lack of empathy, and the insatiable need for validation and control.

Through the detailed exploration of the core features of narcissistic personality disorder, we give ourselves the ability to recognize the harmful patterns and the toxic behaviors that we experience in our life which leads us to take steps to regain our autonomy, self-worth, and freedom to create our life as we like it.

The Grandiose Sense of Self and Entitlement

The central trait of the narcissistic personality is a highly grandiose self-perspective, an internalized perception of superiority, uniqueness, and entitlement to favor and praise. This extravagant self-picture functions like an impenetrable state of mind, protecting the narcissist from feelings of inadequacy, insecurity, and a sense of physical emptiness that lies deep in the self.

Individuals with NPD may have an inflated sense of their skills, success, and value as a person, constantly putting themselves in the spotlight and expecting people to be focused on their needs, wishes, and views above everyone else's. This inflated feeling of self-importance is coupled with an exceptional feeling of their uniqueness, the belief that they are somehow "special" or "entitled" to rewards that most ordinary people don't experience.

These grandiose views of themselves are additionally solidified by a mentality that predisposes them to a sense of entitlement, which is the belief that they deserve special treatment, adulation, and unflinching loyalty from people they come into contact with. This sense of superiority is reflected in a multitude of bad behaviors, from the narcissist's unconditional need for instant gratification without anyone else's permission to his direct disrespect of others' boundaries and autonomy.

The narcissist's exaggerated view of himself and the mentality of being entitled to everything is usually based on deep insecurities and a not real consciousness of self-worth. Behind the mask of pride and incorruptibility lies a thin ego, which always is looking for recognition and admiration from the outside to strengthen its foundations. This insatiable craving for self-admiration and an indescribable need for constantly preserving the mirage of their superiority is what pushes the narcissists to launch an endless endeavor for self-promotion, outdoing others and downgrading anyone who tries to question their highly overrated selves.

The victims of the narcissistic type of abuse are destroyed by the narcissist's grandiose self-esteem and a contemptuous attitude toward the needs, feelings, and boundaries of the people around them. The narcissist's unbending confidence in their supremacy, accompanied by the conviction that they are meant to be treated differently from others, cause them to exploit, manipulate, and in the end, dismiss those who do not live up to their expectations and those who dare to challenge their self-aggrandizement.

It needs to be stressed that the narcissistic grandiose sense of self and entitlement is not the only trait present but rather is a fundament that is vast and underpins the numerous toxic behaviors and emotional abuses that victims have to endure. The knowledge of what fueled this twisted self-image will help us to recognize and tackle the narcissist's seemingly endless want of control, adoration, and validation.

Lack of Empathy and Disregard for Others

Probably the major and severest trait of the narcissistic personality is the lack of empathy and true care for the mood, thoughts, and fate of others. People with NPD have a terrible lack of awareness of the other person's personality. They think of others as objects and treat them according to their personal preferences - to be manipulated, used, and eventually disposed of.

This terrible empathy gap owes to the warped perspective of self-centeredness and their unflinching conviction in their superiority. For them, the requests, lessons, and viewpoints of others are of less significance. Their self-conviction about their rights and desires makes them more important than others. The inability of narcissists to look, listen, and validate the internal world of the people they meet is one of the main characteristics of their emotional and psychological dysfunction, and it is what gives origin to the severe pain and trauma they cause to their victims.

In this cold disrespect to others' humanity, they show toxic behaviors in many ways, from the obvious disregard for their partner's emotional needs to their lack of caring about how their words and actions can affect their beloved partners. They might demonstrate apathy in the situations of others' suffering and may have an indifferent calm or reassurance of the person's experience. In more extreme cases, the narcissist may enjoy the agony and discomfort of other people, they get that distorted kind of pleasure from controlling, changing and eventually damaging the people around them.

The narcissist's profound lack of empathy even extends to their emotional state, thus, making them unable to be in connection with other people or experience the full range of emotions human beings are capable of. Even though they can skillfully simulate emotional outpouring to get what they want, narcissists' inner selves are usually deficient in genuine emotions like intimacy, compassion, or sincerity of feeling. The emotional self-disconnect fuels their inner thought of uniqueness. They cannot grasp the subjective truth about others because they fail to understand their point of view.

For the survivors of the narcissism abuse, this deep feeling of empathy deprivation is more than devastating, to them they are nobody, they are being invalidated and they are alone in their struggles. The inability of a narcissist to truly be attentive and responsive to their partner's emotional needs may result in long-term feelings of being abandoned, ignored, and undervalued, which can lead to an erosion of one's self-value.

Furthermore, the narcissist's disrespect for the authority, space, and autonomy of others reveals itself in a multitude of ways, such as controlling, manipulative, and emotionally abusive behaviors as they aggressively pursue their interests with a complete disregard for others' well-being. This constant loss of human empathy for others is a sign of the pathology of narcissism and the reason behind the enormous pain and trauma that their victims suffer.

In this journey of reclaiming back control from narcissistic abuse, it is important to gain a deeper sense of what such a lack of empathy is and the vast damage it does to all those surrounding this kind of person. We can better identify the toxic patterns, set up the firm boundaries, and eventually, cease to be the narcissist's automatons by realizing the narcissist's emotional coldness, and their fundamental lack of empathy for other people.

Fragile Ego and Need for Constant Validation

At the heart of all the narcissist's exaggerated self-perception and feeling of superiority is a very weak ego that is trying to use all the external validation and praise to hold its damaged walls together. This is where hollow insecurity and a complete lack of genuine self-worth force the narcissist to endlessly seek constant attention, adoration, and complete loyalty and devotion from people around.

Individuals with NPD usually become oversensitive to negative criticism, even if it is meant to be helpful. All egoistic belief in themselves inflated with even the slightest or obvious challenge from others' is reacted with intense defensive reactions like rage, indignation, and subtle forms of revenge or punishment. It is this vulnerability of the narcissist's ego that is a direct manifestation of the low self-esteem and self-loathing that they are desperately trying to conceal from themselves and all others.

The narcissist tries to make up for these hidden insecurities by chasing external validation incessantly and unyieldingly, which ultimately leads to the need for constant praise, admiration, and undying love from anyone surrounding this person. It is possible, for instance, for them to have grandiose displays of achievement, explicitly fishing for either compliments or accolades or to engage in a constant cycle of bragging and self-aggrandizement. Whatever can reveal the hidden weakness of their man-made perfection is met with an aggressive response in a sharp and usually unfriendly manner.

The insatiable urge for validation and adoration also serves as the narcissist's driving force behind an impeccably crafted entourage of those knowingly or unknowingly bolstering the ego, pampering the vanity, and constantly reinforcing the false self-image of the narcissist. These "flying monkeys" as they are usually addressed, become an extension of the narcissist's vulnerable sense of self, providing the constant supply of acting and praise that the narcissist is in such need of.

Sadly, the narcissist's inflated ego and need for instant affirmation of their self-worth too often make them incapable of forming authentic and substantial relationships with others. They tend to have shallow relationships, as the narcissist's main goal is to be praised, and admiration, and the ego-charges validation of their self-perceived superiority. This emotional detachment will make the victims of narcissists feel isolated, unseen, and worthless along with the realization that they will be replaced whenever they don't do what the narcissist has wanted.

This effervescent ego and incessant quest for validation are plastic elements that form the core of this individual's life and how they sees the world. By knowing the bottomlessness of the narcissist's insecurities and their attempt to bolster the hugely damaged self-esteem, we can deal with the poisoned interactions of the phenomenon much better.

So, further along the way of recovery and regaining our lives, strong self-compassion and an appreciation of the depth of our pain due to narcissistic abuse becomes a necessity. The narcissist's fragile narcissistic ego and the need for continuous validation are a main reason we were devalued, worthless, and wondered about our inherent value. Yet, in the course of this transformation we may find the determination to rebuild our life, cut ties with fake connections, and unleash the amazing power that has been lying within ourselves for a very long time.

Exploitative and Manipulative Tendencies

At the core of the narcissistic personality, there is a powerful feeling of entitlement, a deeply rooted belief that the narcissist is born with better qualities, and therefore should be treated specially, adored, and remain extremely loyal to other people. Behind this grandiosity and profound lack of empathy, there is a desire for constant validation and praise, which is the toxic foundation for all exploitative and manipulative behaviors narcissists typically exhibit towards people dear to them and those who are within their orbit.

NPD individuals mostly disregard the limits, needs, and self-autonomy of people, seeing those they interact with as an extension of their ego being used, controlled, and discarded on a whim. The lack of consideration for the humanity of those around them takes different forms, like financial exploitation, resource control, and the ultimate forms of emotional and psychological abuse.

Behind the narcissist's charming, charismatic façade, there is a devious side that is quick to take advantage of circumstances in the quest of being deemed "the perfect" partner, friend, or relative. Such painstakingly created image forms a magnet that pulls in the naïve defenses of the narcissistic addict. Once their victim has been caught, the narcissist's true nature starts shining, through a devoted work that progressively weakens the victim's self-esteem, autonomy, and perception of reality.

One of the most common and most painful forms of mistreatment done by the narcissist is financial abuse. People with NPD are characterized by an unstoppable desire for power, control, and permanent validation of their exceptionalism – and this is the case even if it is necessary to abuse the financial and security resources of their loved ones regrettably.

This financial abuse will cover the whole range, starting from the narcissist's open misuse of their partner's money or belongings up to more clandestine forms of control, such as prohibiting their victim from knowing about finances or making their partner vulnerable to losing their employment. In the most extreme cases, the narcissist may embezzle, lie, or destroy the financial resources of their victim without reservation – only to serve the grandiose illusions and sense of entitlement.

However, apart from money, the exploitative tactics of a narcissist also cause pain in areas such as emotions, psychology, and bodily well-being. The narcissist affirms their supremacy by gaslighting, emotional mistreatment, and undermining the self-esteem of their victim, which is the first step of bringing down their prey to create a toxic cycle of abuse and dominance.

Sadly, the narcissist's exploitative attitude is based on this enormous sense of entitlement and contempt toward the personhood of people close to them. Those perpetrators do not perceive their victims as unique individuals entitled to respect and dignity, but rather as sources of endless exploitation, as the only justification for their inflated self-importance.

On our journey to regaining our lives from narcissistic abuse, it is of prime importance to understand how narcissists exploit and manipulate people. This understanding will not only help us to become aware of how these harmful patterns infiltrate our own lives but will also help us to build the tools and strategies needed to protect ourselves and those we love from the destructive fallout of the narcissist's toxic.

The Spectrum of Narcissistic Traits

It is critical to comprehend that Narcissistic Personality Disorder (NPD) stretches on a spectrum with individuals showing various degrees of the characteristic traits and behaviors that reflect this multifaceted and seriously damaging condition. While some narcissists may show a more explicit, grandiosity form of the disorder, others could present with the more covert and/or "vulnerable" narcissistic style – hiding their entitled and superior sense under the mask of a fragile victim humbles themselves.

The reality, however, is that – irrespective of the manifestations – the core of narcissism is the distorted self-perception together with the lack of empathy and unslakable desire for validating and controlling people end up having the lives of the people taken hostage by the narcissist, utterly destroyed.

The outright grandiose, narcissist usually boasts a flamboyant quite excessive picture of self-importance that has been ignored or slighted by society. There is no apology for such a victim's thinking, behavior, and attitude. This kind of person is arrogant. These types of people may be engaged with harassment, swindling, and emotional abuse, at the same time without any shame or care for the outcomes of their acts.

Rather than the overtly apparent and dramatic narcissism usually associated with the disorder, the covert or "vulnerable" narcissist may present a more subtle and insidious form, shielding their strong and entitled sense of self with a veil of fragility, victimhood, and a need to constantly receive sympathy and feedback. Compared to the blatant elitism and oppression that are evident in their grandiose peers, these people may exhibit less apparent signs of aggression or exploitation, albeit they are equally, if not more, damaging, since many times, they use passive-aggressive behaviors, emotional manipulation, and the constant need for attention.

A weak-willed narcissist might appear overly shy and insecure, and quite easily offended, so they use their obvious weaknesses to get sympathy and special treatment from those around them. They can be needy and require a lot of validation and reassurance. At the same time, they can be critical of people who do not satisfy their insatiable need for constant admiration. This surreptitious form of narcissism is especially deceitful because it covers up the feelings of entitlement and contempt towards other people with a mask of emotional fragility and victim mentality.

No matter what form the Narcissistic personality may take, the fundamental characteristics that make it what it remains: are the reckless ego, the absence of empathy, the ego vulnerability, and the exploiting and manipulating surroundings. These ego-grandiose, whether blatantly ostentatious or secretly helpless, all have a common self-distortion and an unyielding need for power, and control, and chronically sanction their sense of superiority.

It is useful to realize that this range of narcissistic traits makes us able to identify and master the different and often complex manifestations of that deep pathologic disorder. When the features of narcissism are identified and understood, people acquire the ability to spot the toxic patterns and behaviors that have trodden upon their own lives and take the appropriate measures to reclaim their independence, their self-esteem, and the freedom to build their own lives.

In our journey toward mental and emotional healing, let us approach this understanding of personality disorder with a sharp eye, an intelligent mind, and an inexhaustible supply of compassion – for the victims of this type of abuse, as well as for the people that become victims to the distorted logic of narcissistic mindset. By doing this, we enable ourselves to follow a more comprehensive, empathy-based, and ultimately more successful route, which leads us to the recovery and regaining of our well-earned place in this world.

Chapter 2: Narcissistic Traits and Behaviors: Red Flags to Watch For

One of the crucial aspects of our path to regaining control over our lives from narcissistic abuse is understanding and recognizing the specific narcissistic personality traits. Through the training of our ability to see and understand these toxic patterns, we help ourselves to be able to more skillfully perceive, negotiate, and ultimately overcome the negative influence of the narcissist.

During this chapter, we will consider narcissism's complex facets, allowing us to unravel the complex web of charm, manipulation, and the emotional carnage twined around the unsuspecting subjects of narcissism. We will not only cover the deliberately created impression of openness and the demand for admiration and domination but also investigate the multifaceted red flags that give a hint of the narcissist's true dark character.

Armed with this knowledge, not only do we take care of ourselves, but we also grow to become discerning and resilient in supporting others who possibly are going through the effects of narcissistic abuse. Thus, let us sail into this exploration with open eyes, undeniable courage, and firm decision to not only regain our lives but also our power and rightfully take our place in the world.

Charming and Charismatic Façade

The mask that a narcissist shows in society is the most horrible and insidious because of its capability to deceive with charm, empathy, and charisma. This image of perfection draws the unsuspecting victim into the trap of the narcissist, where the true nature of the person is hidden, behind the perverted core which lies underneath the surface.

At the start of a relationship, the narcissist could be the "ideal" partner, friend, or family member who appears to be diligent, engaging, and filled with empathy and care about the lives of others. They do this by drenching their victims with material displays of affection, grand romantic actions, and endless uncountable praises and compliments.

This veneer of good intentions is, in fact, a cunning strategy and is used to bypass the critical, rational facilities of the victims and strike the deepest recesses of their hearts and minds. The narcissist comprehends, always at a deeper level, that the more they portray themselves as perfect, the easier it is for them to attract their prey and then keep them on a string of emotional manipulation and power by the end.

Sadly, this polished and amiable front is just a carefully crafted veil, nothing but a tool to hide the true essence of the narcissist which is very often characterized by cold-heartedness, ruthlessness, and utter lack of empathy. Under the cover, they have extreme feelings of entitledness, an insatiable need for status and appreciation, and a lack of respect for the personal space of the people around them.

Indeed, along the way, the deception starts to wear off, and the charisma turns out to be a mere facade for the real bile of the narcissistic personality that lies within. These same qualities that lured the likely victim - the attentiveness, the affection, the never-ending flow of compliments and adoration – later on become the main tools that the narcissist uses to control, and manipulate the victim's emotions, and gradually destroy the self-esteem.

It should be acknowledged that this appealing and pleasant facade serves as a medium of self-expression for the narcissist which is rooted in the narcissist's psychology. Narcissists can camouflage profound insecurities, lack of empathy, and basically, their feelings of unworthiness by portraying themselves as the incarnation of the "perfect" partner or mate.

We must keep our awareness high regarding this charming camouflage because it is the first and mightiest weapon that the narcissist uses against us. By strengthening our discerning skills and the ability to resist the narcissist's fake persona, we get empowered to decide with self-control, set strong boundaries, and defend ourselves from the narcissist's destructive behaviors in the end.

Constant Need for Admiration and Attention

The core of the narcissistic personality is the never-ending hunger for appreciation, attention, and validation of one's overwhelming self-worth. This continuous hunger for external approval is the central theme of NPD compelling the narcissist to be involved in countless attention-seeking behaviors and manipulative tactics intended to serve the cause of soothing their fragile ego and consolidating their superiority over other people.

People who have traits of narcissism often have an actual need to be the center of attention, hence their continuous search for avenues to demonstrate their abilities, achievements, and claimed uniqueness. They may dominate talks, they may think of themselves and blow their own trumpet and fish for compliments and praise and are unable to bear even the slightest deviation in adoration and validation that they desperately need.

The need for attention and recognition, which is not only a superficial issue, defines the narcissist's deep-seated sense of inadequacy and lack of sincere self-esteem. Within the ostentation of bravado and importance, there is a weak ego, which keeps on demanding external recognition to maintain its crumbling walls. The narcissist's ceaseless yearning for admiration and adoration is a disguise for the fact that they feel no self-esteem at all, and they have an enormous void inside.

Unfortunately, the true motive of narcissists, which is the craving for admiration, precedes any authentic connection with others. Lack of emotional intimacy usually defines the relationships of narcissists, because they are looking for ways to get endless praise, confirmation, and reinforcement for their greatness above all else. The loved ones of the narcissist are forced to give up their needs, limits, and autonomy so that the narcissist may feel satisfied with being in the spotlight. This often leads to a sense of chronic loneliness, invalidation, and emotional starvation in those in the narcissist's orbit.

Additionally, the narcissist's "worship" might have more visible behavioral consequences like disturbing social events and conversations specifically to make these all about the narcissist or even to sabotage someone else's success and accomplishments. Any action that has the potential to damage the narcissist's place in the spotlight or to argue over their supremacy will be met with a quick, in some cases even hostile, response.

While the road to recovery from narcissistic abuse may seem long, if we stay mindful of such attention-seeking behaviors and the deep-rooted need for admiration underneath them, we will be able, eventually, to gain the upper hand in this conflict and move on. They will go as far as manipulation and if not careful people around them will suffer from their ugly games.

Envious and Resentful of Others' Successes

Along with the narcissist's desperation to have recognition and validation around the clock, there is an underlying feeling of envy and resentment for the perceived accomplishments and successes of others. Such deep-seated jealousy and bitter resentment towards the good fortune and amazing characteristics of others is a main feature of a narcissistic personality and is manifested in a broad spectrum of negative behavior that is ultimately directed against the victims of their envy.

The key to narcissist's envy is the profound sense of inadequacy and the deep-seated idea of their own extraordinary. The self-grandeur and the misplaced sense of entitlement of a narcissist results in a view of the world through a filter of competition, where any success or positive attribute of others is seen as a threat to their supremacy.

Such resentment and envy can be manifested in different ways, from the narcissist's blatant dismissal or devaluation of their spouse or loved ones to an overt type of undermining. The narcissist will try to use subtle put-downs, passive-aggressive comments, or even outright efforts of trying to discredit or devalue your success to maintain his/her false and over-inflated sense of being superior as well as to douse the fears of inadequacy that threaten to overwhelm him/her.

For the intimate relationship context, this envious and resentful behavior is particularly destructive, as the narcissist interprets the independent sources of fulfillment, or successes, of the partner as a direct attack on their dominance and control. The narcissist can actively be working to disrupt their partner's career goals, hobbies, and social network deliberately to keep the partner feeling dependent, small, and completely under the narcissist's influence.

Besides, a narcissist's resentment of others' success can be even broader, directed at anyone that they believe to be superior to themselves, regardless of whether it is their friends or strangers. The constant feeling of envy in a narcissistic person prompts him or her to gossip, character assassination, and even open attacks on the success and reputation of his or her competitors.

However, the envy and jealousy of successful narcissistic people is not anything odd or funny, but rather it is a fundamental aspect of their distorted world outlook, and it is one of the leading factors of their most toxic and damaging behaviors. Grasping the fundamentals of the depths of a narcissist's insatiable jealousy that are evident in their desperate attempts to maintain their imaginary superiority can help us in the navigation of their manipulative behavior to safeguard our well-being as well as the integrity of our relationship.

The road to recovery from narcissistic abuse is a path embellished with compassion, we should develop a meaningful sense of compassion not only for ourselves and our loved ones but also for the complex and mostly wounded people who are now trapped in the narcissistic mindset. However, when our empathic understanding would be able to end the circle of resentment, envy, and the ultimate domination through which the narcissist's toxic behavior is rooted.

Sense of Entitlement and Lack of Accountability

One of the most detrimental and the most enduring characteristic of the narcissistic personality is their inclination toward being entitled to everything and being fully irresponsible for their actions and the lives of others as well as for themselves. This distorted perception is in essence the cause of their toxic behaviors; the narcissist is driven by their strong need to be better than anyone else, to receive special treatment, and to have their grandiose self-esteem all the time.

Narcissistic individuals often act in a very shocking way, without any concern for the boundaries, needs, and the right of others to be independent; to them, the people around them are just a reflection of their ego which they can use, manipulate, and dispose of when they see fit. It appears in many forms, from simple neglect of the emotional needs of the partners and the close ones to a more organized abuse of their resources and the gradual establishment of control over their behavior and independence.

One of the main features of a narcissist's distorted personality is their profound inability to take responsibility. They endlessly find excuses for themselves, blame others, and get into reasoning and victim-blaming to avoid being responsible for the pain, they have caused their victims. In the narcissist perverted worldview, they are always the victim, always a target of the incompetence, malice, or inadequacies of others - it is a narrative they cannot do without to maintain and reinforce the perception.

Such a sense of entitlement and lack of accountability is likely to be more destructive in an intimate relationship setting, where the narcissist's ruthless pursuit of control and validation is commonly at the cost of the wellbeing, autonomy, and basic dignity guaranteeing of the partner. The narcissist may include a range of abusive behaviors, from financial exploitation and resource control to emotional manipulation and systematic elimination of the person's self-worth realization, all the while denying their responsibility for the damage made.

Unfortunately, narcissistic entitlement and lack of accountability are not just the means of the narcissist, but rather their traits that help to manifest their destructive behaviors and to feel superior to others around them. This distorted belief in their entitlement to special privileges in addition to disregarding the consequences of their actions creates extremely dense character armor that prevents the narcissist from experiencing sincere remorse or the meaningful change that would be necessary to fix the cycle of violence.

In the continuation of my journey towards restoring my life from narcissistic abuse, it is of prime importance to develop a thorough knowledge of this sense of entitlement and lack of responsibility that is embodied in the narcissistic character. With the knowledge and awareness of the toxic traits and ways they manifest, we empower ourselves to navigate more effectively the narcissist's manipulations, set proper boundaries, and ultimately, save ourselves and our loved ones from the destruction of their abusive behaviors.

Exploitative and Controlling Behaviors

The main characteristic of a narcissistic personality is the sense of entitlement. This means the person feels they are better than others and should always be treated special, receiving excessive admiration and loyalty from people around them. The feeling of superiority, combined with a lack of empathy and constant need for affirmation characterizes the exploitative and controlling behavior in narcissists; these toxic actions are at center stage destroying loved ones as well as people who fall under their sphere's influence.

People having narcissistic tendencies frequently show a surprising lack of respect for others' limits, requirements, and freedom. They perceive those in their life as mere continuations of themselves – something to be utilized, maneuvered with, and thrown away whenever convenient. This heartless disregard for the humanness of people around them can be seen in various ways such as financial exploitation or controlling resources up until less obvious methods like emotional abuse and psychological manipulation.

Usually, the narcissist has a character that is charming and charismatic. They create this image to appear kind, giving, and always correct in being someone's partner, friend, or family member. This attractive personality acts like a strong magnet that pulls innocent individuals toward their trap for manipulation and dominance. When they have trapped someone, the real identity of a narcissist comes out as they make efforts to destroy the self-confidence, independence, and understanding of their victim.

Financial abuse, a type of manipulation that happens to many people, can be particularly damaging when done by someone with NPD. This is because individuals who display Narcissistic Personality Disorder frequently show traits such as an insatiable hunger for power and control along with the constant requirement for validation of their supposed superiority - and they will not hesitate to use any tactics necessary to maintain this feeling of dominance; even if it entails exploiting the financial assets and stability within relationships they share.

The type of abuse that occurs in a relationship with a narcissist is not limited to emotional and physical harm. Often, these individuals also exploit their partners financially for personal gain at the cost of their victim's well-being. This exploitation can happen in many ways: from simply using up all the partner's income or assets without any concern for future needs; to more hidden methods like restricting access to financial details or purposely making it difficult for the victim to find and keep work. In severe situations, theft might happen directly by stealing money or property, committing frauds related to finances, or draining off savings systematically along with resources – all actions done by narcissists driven solely by their self-centered motives and exaggerated feelings of deservingness.

Likewise, the narcissist's tendency to exploit can go much further than just money matters. They may dominantly control not only the financial side but also the emotional, psychological, and even physical condition of people in their lives by frequently using gaslighting, emotional mistreatment and slowly wearing down self-value. The narcissist wants to show power over others, keep up their supremacy, and continue the harmful pattern of reliance and domination through these methods.

Tragically, the narcissist's exploitative nature is frequently supported by an intense belief in entitlement and a total lack of concern for the human value of those close to them. They don't see their dear ones as independent persons who should have honor and worthiness, but instead treat them like objects that can be used to fulfill personal benefits and maintain a constant glorification of their exaggerated self-perception.

While we move ahead on this path to take back our lives from the hold of narcissistic abuse, it becomes very important that we gain a thorough comprehension of how narcissists exploit and dominate. This knowledge is crucial not just for recognizing harmful routines within our own lives, but also for creating necessary instruments and methods to safeguard against dangers posed by toxic behaviors typical of those with narcissistic traits.

Gaslighting and Emotional Invalidation

One of the most devastating and terrible qualities of narcissistic personalities is the narcissist's constant use of gaslighting and emotional invalidation as a method to assert power, undermine their victims' reality, and reinforce their falsely superior thinking. These deadly weapons that a narcissist relies on, aim at exploiting self-doubts, self-value, and the very essence of truth – all for the narcissist to attain power and control.

Gaslighting, a term originating from a famous 1944 movie whose name is "Gaslight", is a variety of psychological abuse in which the narcissist continuously and persuasively denies the victim's perceptions, feelings, and memories, leading the victim to think that he/she is crazy. The narcissist uses a merciless continuous flow of lies, denials, and distortions to confusingly and dependently make the victim weaker and more susceptible to the manipulations of the narcissist.

Besides the gaslighting, the narcissist will often deploy the tactic called emotional invalidation. It involves ignoring, dismissing, or diminishing the feelings, needs, or experiences of their victim. Through methodically destroying their partner's or loved one's emotional landscape by disregarding and dismissing it, the narcissist gains the confidence to erode further their victim's self-esteem, their basic right to have their feelings acknowledged, and their capacity to rely on their intuitions and perceptions.

Unfortunately, the traumatic effects of disillusionment and emotional damage could hardly be underestimated. With each passing day, the narcissist's toxic behavior continues to wear away the victim's trust in self and thereby leads the victim to believe more than ever in the narcissist's distorted perception of reality. They might start to doubt themselves, second-guess their memories and sensations and eventually merge with the narcissist's twisted storyline – a traumatic crisis that could influence all aspects of their mental health and being for so long.

It is important to understand that such gaslighting and invalidation were not so many isolated occurrences, or even a few characteristic events of the narcissist's behavior, but rather fundamental pieces of their psychological makeup and relentless pursuit of domination and control. By recognizing the crafty nature of these techniques which in the end gives them an enormous hold on their victim, we can identify the tell-tale signs, exercise firm boundaries, and put an end to the narcissist's influence over us.

As our journey of regaining what has been lost to narcissistic abuse, we need to view gaslighting and feelings of invalidation with vigilance, a discerning mind, deep well of compassion that spans to our loved ones, and who are also narcissistic victims in the deep-seated interior of the mind. We opt for a way that is more multi-dimensional, expansive, and effective for us to return to our rightful place of respect, value, and belonging in the world.

Intermittent Displays of Affection (the "Seesaw")

The most confounding and emotionally shattering thing about the narcissistic personality is the narcissist's habit of periodically showing compassion and withdrawing emotionally. This is a dangerous pattern that has become known as the "seesaw" or "push-pull" dynamic. This inconsistent and unstable emotional topography becomes the means of manipulating and controlling their victims, and the victims remain in an endless state of confusion, anxiety, and hopelessness as they long for the narcissist's attention and approval.

In the very beginning, the narcissist is likely to make the receiver of their attention feel excessively loved, appreciated, and adored. They could be too good to be true, overly affectionate, and too much into physical and emotional intimacy. As the starting point of the "love bombing," the narcissist expertly maneuvers the prey into a profound emotional state encompassed by a powerful sense of belonging, connection, and finally, the validation of the victim's inner worthiness.

Nevertheless, this hardly lasts because the narcissist's real self starts to shine through. The narcissist may withdraw without notice, of the affection, emotional engagement, and source of validation, leaving the victim at a point of deep confusion, hurt, and desperate to regain the favor of the narcissist. The pattern of unpredictable reinforcement is actively utilized by the narcissist to keep the victim off-balance. The intermittent alternation between displays of affection and rejection is merely part of the manipulation strategy to make the victim keep seeking to please the narcissist.

Nevertheless, this "seesaw" is not only a trivial anomaly of narcissistic personality, but rather it is a sly and effective manipulative mechanism to establish dominance and to control their victims. Through executing such emotional ups and downs to his partner or loved one, the narcissist can be able to exploit one's deepest weaknesses, destroy one's self-image, and make sure that he/she remains dependent upon the narcissist's approval and validation.

Additionally, the swinging between the affection and withdrawal pattern can seriously affect the victim's mental and emotional health and function adversely. Living life in a continuous state of insecurity, the desire for the narcissist's attention that never arrives, and the wear of the victim's personality and self-esteem can lead to many health problems like anxiety, depression, stress, and even PTSD.

As we move through the difficult road of closing the claws of narcissistic abuse, it becomes crucial that we develop a solid grasp of the "seesaw" mechanism as well as the various toxic patterns that support it. Through the observance of love-bombing, emotional withdrawal, and the narcissist's unyielding need to assert and maintain control, we can empower ourselves enough to become immune to the fake expressions of affection, set healthy boundaries, and eventually be able to liberate ourselves of the emotional chaos that the narcissist has kept us locked up in.

Through this enhanced state of consciousness and the development of emotional resilience, lie the keys to our emancipation, restoration of autonomy, and reclamation of our rightful place in this world – no longer held hostage by the narcissist's indiscriminate and manipulative emotional landscape, we rediscover our true selves, led by the certainty that we are deserving of unconditional.

Chapter 3: The Narcissist's Playbook: Manipulation Tactics Exposed

While it is crucial to understand that we are on a journey of reclaiming our lives from the clutches of narcissistic abuse, it is equally imperative that we go deeper into the manifold ways in which narcissists use their arsenal of weaponry: the persistent and sometimes subtle instruments that they employ as they seek to dominate, undermine, and ultimately hold you in a tight grip.

The textbook of a narcissist is a multifaceted web made of poisonous behaviors, each of them being carefully designed and intertwined to secure the narcissist's twisted perception of their greatness and entitlement. From the charming coercions often labeled as love-bombing and hoovering, to the coldly calculated destruction of our supporters and worst, the weaponization of even our nearest and dearest, the narcissist's manipulative tools are very personal and are geared towards stripping us of our agency, our self-worth, and our very senses of reality.

Through exposure to these subtle tactics, we can better apprehend signals, and establish clear boundaries, and in the long run, we can recover and regain the power that was purposefully stripped. Therefore, let us explore the narcissist's playbook with determined bravery, a critical eye, and the unshakable certainty that our survival and freedom are well in our hands.

Hoovering and Love-Bombing

While it is crucial to understand that we are on a journey of reclaiming our lives from the clutches of narcissistic abuse, it is equally imperative that we go deeper into the manifold ways in which narcissists use their arsenal of weaponry: the persistent and sometimes subtle instruments that they employ as they seek to dominate, undermine, and ultimately hold you in a tight grip.

The textbook of a narcissist is a multifaceted web made of poisonous behaviors, each of them is carefully designed and intertwined to secure the narcissist's twisted perception of their greatness and entitlement. From the charming coercions often labeled as love-bombing and hoovering, to the coldly calculated destruction of our supporters and worst, the weaponization of even our nearest and dearest, the narcissist's manipulative tools are very personal and are geared towards stripping us of our agency, our self-worth, and our very senses of reality.

Through exposure to these subtle tactics, we can better apprehend signals, and establish clear boundaries, and in the long run, we can recover and regain the power that was purposefully stripped. Therefore, let us explore the narcissist's playbook with determined bravery, a critical eye, and the unshakable certainty that our survival and freedom are well in our hands.

This is the time when the cycle of hoovering starts. Because they realize that the victim is emotionally vulnerable and dependent on them, narcissists recognize their victim's weakness. By bombarding their victim with promises, apologies, and what seems like a pure display of remorse, the narcissist attempt to reel their prey back at them again, mostly by reminding the victim about the affection they shared during the "love bombing" phase which usually triggers the victim's hope and regains their trust.

This process of the cyberstalkers' hoovering and love-bombing is so accurately calculated and functioning as such an effective tool for controlling and dominating their targets. The narcissist achieves this by manipulating their victims' deepest weaknesses, so they develop self-esteem issues, and their dependency on the narcissist's approval and affirmation gets reinforced.

Awareness is a key component in fighting narcissistic abuse and hence we should learn about the underlying control mechanisms and the designs that the narcissists use to manipulate. The awareness of the love-bombing, emotional distancing and an insatiable desire to hoover a narcissist takes us to an informed standpoint on how resisting false gestures of affection, drawing boundaries and a release from emotional distress becomes palpable.

Smear Campaigns and Character Assassinations

But the most dangerous and all-encompassing weapon from the narcissist's bag of tricks is the endless, persistent smear campaign and character assassination. Their purpose is to destroy our credibility, leaving us isolated from our support systems for the narcissist to consolidate authority, control, and power.

At the core of the narcissist's slander campaign lies a major fear – a terror of being uncovered, of losing the love and regard that they so helplessly seek, and of giving in the fiction of their perfection and superiority. To feed their fragile ego and win this perceived battle, the narcissist will ruthlessly unleash a 'weapon of mass destruction'- a campaign of lies, distortions, and character assassinations- aimed at making others believe the lies.

This evil method may become manifest in different ways, from the narcissist's direct lies and slanders to their more insidious actions of undermining your character and integrity through gaslighting, doubts, and designs. The narcissist may also involve the "flying monkeys" – the friends, family, and associates who end up serving the agenda of the narcissist in destroying the victim. Therefore, rather than just being a victim, the victim is further isolated and betrayed.

Unfortunately, the consequences of these media offensives may often be both long-reaching and overwhelmingly severe. When the abuser begins to tell lies and exaggerate things, we might start to feel more and more isolated, our reputation tainted and our support system damaged. It could result in quite a strong feeling of betrayal and self-doubt, where the very foundations of our self-worth and personality are broken.

Not only that, but a narcissist's unyielding character assassinations can reach far beyond personal relationships, affecting our professional and social stance, which may even include losing a job or denial of attention from necessary services or resources. The fact that the narcissist would do everything in their power to remain in control and dominate is disturbing, the depths of which show the extent of their depravity.

In the winding trail of the narcissist's smear campaigns, we need to develop a sound sense of this pernicious tactic and the psychosocial factors that motivate it. By understanding that a narcissist's goal is to control the narrative, despite being exposed, and have no respect for the humanity of the victims, we can become more prepared to resist the urge to challenge the truth, and it is an additional step towards claiming our right place in the world.

Besides, having a close circle of allies and supporters–the people who can listen to us validate our experiences, and defend us against the relentless attacks of the narcissist's campaign of smear is very important. Through this fertilization of self-empowering bonds and refusing to be victimized by the narcissist's desolation strategy, we reclaim our status, our autonomy, and our right to be both heard and believed.

Triangulation and Division of Loved Ones

Another powerful and destructive victim manipulation strategy of the narcissist is triangulation – the deliberate and successful use of the relationships and connections that are the most vital to the victim's support system and well-being.

Fundamentally, triangulation is an emotional and psychological form of abuse in which the narcissist deliberately takes the third party position between the existing relationships and dynamics of their victim to incite conflict, thus making that person not only afraid of the narcissist but also the third party involved. This way, the narcissist becomes more dominant and no one can go against the narcissist very easily.

These negative tactics can express themselves through various ways, such as rudeness and obvious jealousy in front of family members and friends, or use less obvious but equally strong tactics, in which the narcissist can undermine the trust and intimacy in their victim's closest relationships. Narcissists can engage in a merciless campaign of lies and distortions, aiming to break the ties that bind the love and trustworthiness of the victim to the very people who would otherwise provide vital emotional support and validation to the victim.

Despite the fact triangulation is hurtful, it is far-reaching and can be painfully destructive. The narcissist continuously creates a web of lies and division. The victim of these lies may find themselves quickly isolated, the support systems they had counted on are systematically torn down and their sense of belonging and self-worth have been shaken. This can be a tragedy that a soldier has to go through a spiritual crisis, abandonment, the core of his personality, and the experience of himself being shattered.

The narcissist's strategies of triangulation may not only give rise to feelings of deep suspicion and distrust but also to a mental state in which one is not capable of properly appreciating the value of close and caring relationships that are required to heal the victim and make him/her resilient.

However, narcissist's fondness for turning the victim's confidants against the victim is clear evidence of the depth of their wickedness and the level of authority they hold over victims. Through destroying the victim's support network and provoking conflicts between the closest relationships, the narcissist's goal is to make the victim completely dependent, lonely, and prevailing, thus making them easily achievable.

On our way to encountering the narcissist's triangulation triage, we must have a complete grasp of this toxic scheme and the underlying psychological bases that operate its actuation. Through an understanding of the narcissist's anxious need to maintain control over the narrative, their deep-seated fear of being exposed, and their total disregard for the welfare of their victims, we can more effectively defend ourselves against their enticing lies, stand firm on our truth, and finally rebellion against their manipulation to regain the nurturing relationships and support systems that enhance our recovery.

That aside, it is also as important that we embark on this path with a spirit of relentless kindness- towards ourselves, and our loved ones, who have been in the cross-hairs of the narcissist's games. Through facilitating open communication, applying strict limits, and continually striving to rebuild the broken trust and the intimacy that was destroyed, we can reclaim the power of our most valuable relationships, and so we can be able to construct a strong base in which the foundations for our future well-being and resilience will be built.

Financial Abuse and Resource Control

One of the most treacherous and unsparing tools that narcissists use is mercilessly and cunningly grooming their victim on a financial level by taking hold of their money and security order – a vicious technique that leads to an increasing dependence of the victim on the narcissist and his whims.

Financial abuse, an overarching and normally unrecognized part of narcissistic abuse, incorporates various inappropriate manifestations, from the unequivocal misuse and even stealing of the victim's income, assets, and belongings to the more subtle forms of control and manipulation that limit the victim's accessibility of financial information and their capability to acquire personal financial independence.

Narcissistic financial control is what ignites the narcissist to exploit their victims, recognizing that the ultimate goal is to rob them of their financial independence so that he or she be able to control them, diminish their self-respect, and thereby create and prolong the cycle of dependency that is critical in all the narcissistic relationships.

The narcissist may employ different methods of manipulation. Such actions may include but are not limited to depriving the victim of employment opportunities, denying them access to financial resources, or complete lack of responsibility for the victim's well-being.

Regrettably, the adverse effects of this financial abuse might be both wide-ranging and utterly devastating leaving the victim in a state of insecurity, stress, and loss of wholeness. Victims without material resources to support their needs, plan for the future, and escape the narcissist's influence might be forced into a financially dependent web, unable to see a clear road to independence and self-sufficiency.

This is not only a financial problem, but also a psychological and emotional one as the victim faces feelings of shame, guilt, and loss of their self-esteem and autonomy. The narcissist seeks to derail the victim's financial situation by any means necessary and leave them bankrupt and powerless. This will take away the victim's trust in their own decisions and make them feel isolated resulting in the victim being unable to break free from the grip of the narcissist without support.

Throughout the financial manipulation of the narcissist, we have to develop a solid understanding of this narcissistic maneuver and the psychological factors that are its driving forces. By identifying the narcissist's insatiable quest for control, total lack of concern for the victims, and the potentially disastrous effects of these financial abuses, we are in a better place to fight against their manipulative tactics, obtain the necessary resources and support needed, and ultimately, regain our financial freedom and the basis of our future success.

Besides, we must confront this process with undeviating compassion towards those who, maybe, are affected by the narcissist's financial abuse, not only us. Through organizing a supportive and uplifting community, we can accomplish jointly the destruction of the shame and stigma that so frequently come together with financial abuse, and the release of the victims from financial insecurity and enable them to start a new life.

Isolation and Cutting Off Support Systems

The goal of pathological narcissists' manipulating tactics, which can be quite disturbing, is a systemic isolation of the target whereby he/she cuts off the victim's network of supporters, thus the victim is fully under the control of the narcissist.

This tactic can even be said to have two purposes for the narcissist: firstly, it is used to keep the victim feeling weak and helpless; and secondly, it is used to effectively block the victim from gaining influence or connections as well as the very validation sources that would otherwise help in defeating the narcissist's influence and regaining one's autonomy.

The narcissist's pathological manipulation to isolate their perfect from their outside social environments may present itself in many ways, from the more flagrant behaviors like undermining the family and friends relations of the prey, to the more subtle ways of emotional and psychological abuse that progressively deteriorate the victim's social support systems.

The Narcissist through the calculated use of lies, character assassinations, and the strategic manipulation of their victim's inmost fears and insecurities attempts to pull apart or destroy these bonds between two persons, which could otherwise manage to keep their victim afloat or in contact with the reality. They may make their victim to such an extent that their victim would be isolated physically and this isolation may limit the victim's freedom of movement, communication, and the basic needs a victim needs to try to sustain those connections and seek help.

Regrettably, this isolation can be not only reaching and emotionally destructive but also profoundly damaging, leaving the victim feeling entirely lonely, abandoned, and deprived of the emotional nurturance and material supports that most usually greatly contribute to their well-being as well as their inner strength to resist incessant abuses of the narcissist.

In the absence of this trustworthy support system, the victim's resilience may diminish with the narcissist's ability to gaslight, emotionally manipulate, and erode the victim's self-worth and autonomy. The isolation methods employed by narcissists aim to magnify the victim's dependence, insecurity, and deep-seated belief that they can no longer run away from the narcissist's influence.

While dealing with this malevolent tool of the narcissist, we must continue to stand strong with absolute dedication to restructuring the broken systems that the narcissist has instigated to destroy. This may imply the tough and necessary work of restoring torn relationships, defining clear borders, and growing new sources of nourishment and approval – all while dealing with the intricate emotional landscape of deceit, distrust, and the remaining effects of the narcissist's manipulation.

Additionally, it is important to understand within us, that even amid such a profound isolation, there is an inherent power and strength. When we tap into our strength of courage and self-compassion, and that we are full of love, connection, and independence, we start to retrieve the vital support systems that will help to break the control of the narcissist and decide our future.

Threats, Intimidation, and Physical Abuse

The narcissist's arsenal of abusiveness reaches its climax with the most dangerous weapon of threats, intimidation, and outright physical violence – this trio essentially erases any feelings of safety, self-determination, and possibility to fight the narcissist, at least in the victim's perception.

This may be the case of a person who gets in contact with the extent that the narcissist is ready to do anything that will cause physical and emotional pain, including torture. This experience stays with the victim forever since it may take years, even decades, to recover from it.

The readiness of narcissists to make threats, intimidate, and even use violence is usually connected with how far they are willing to go to borrow the weapons of control and superiority. Narcissists may be able to take abusive actions or engage in criminal activities but understanding their potential to do so is a significant step in meaningfully acknowledging the threat and acts in taking protective measures.

The narcissist becomes continuously unrelenting, and he expresses his intentions directly, makes threatening gestures to the victim, and even uses violence to crack down on the victim's sense of security, generate fear, and at last, destroy the individual's will to resist. The emotional arsenal of abuse here can be everything from a verbal rant to destruction of property, to the heartbreaking reality of physical assault or even attempted murder.

For the victim, these threats and acts of violence could cut all the foundation of the world under his or her feet, making him or her have no self-esteem, no trust, and no will to survive. The aftermath of the brutality of the narcissist can be exhibited in many ways which range from debilitating anxiety and post-traumatic stress disorder (PTSD) to the depths of hopelessness and belief that they are powerless against the narcissist.

In the face of this outstanding horror, the victim must become aware of the critical and urgent threat they are exposed to, and take all the required actions to ensure their safety and wellness. It could include obtaining law assistance, requesting restraining orders, and possibly the hardest, but critical, decision of leaving the abusive environment for good.

It is a cruel irony indeed that those who have suffered the narcissist's most extreme and violent forms of abuse, which often lead them to a web of shame, self-doubt, and reluctance to seek the help they so much need, find themselves in this situation. The narcissist's terrorizing campaign and the victim's self-blame that they may have brought about the abuse on themselves can in turn become barriers to availing the necessary resources and intervention that may in the end save their life.

We should be resolute in the face of this most distressing aspect of the narcissist's playbook. Thus it will be imperative that we feel empathy for both ourselves and the people who have endured the angry cruelty of the narcissist. By breaking that silent barrier that usually surrounds these criminal acts, we provide the victims with a platform for talking about the issue, voicing their concerns, and asking for all the support they might need for the road to recovery to begin.

What is crucial is that we campaign for greater legal shields, stronger assistance systems, and society's substantial awareness of the issue of domestic violence and abuse. Only by confronting this crisis, and by providing the infrastructures and resources required to protect victims from any further harm can the future where the narcissist's reign of terror may be washed away be created.

Weaponizing Children and Other Family Members

The narcissist is adept in using and weaponizing children and other family members as one of the most detestable and destructive tools in his repertoire. Feeding their insatiable hunger for dominion and complete disregard for others' welfare, narcissists unhesitatingly employ their loved ones to circumvent their manipulative strategies.

Narcissists can abuse their children in more than one way from emotional and psychological to direct physical cruelty. The children might be made to spend most of their time with the other parent to be able to play this role. During a custody battle, the narcissist won't hesitate to make false accusations of abuse or neglect against the victim thus further ruining the victim's image and portraying himself/herself as the victim.

Apart from their children, narcissists might oppress and exploit other family members, for instance, elderly parents or disabled relatives, as a way of maintaining power and control over the victim. For instance, they might deny essential care or resources to those whom they consider their vulnerable hostages and exploit them for their abusive agenda.

The levels of emotional suffering experienced by children and other family members who are exposed to narcissists' manipulation may go deep and long. They may end as the pawns in the narcissist's game, where they would most likely choose the sides just to avoid the narcissist's wrath when they fail to follow the narcissist's instructions.

The victims of this kind of abuse most often find themselves in a desperate situation, which is between the need to save their loved ones and a terrifying fear of a narcissist's revenge. The revelation that the narcissist uses children and other relatives as a weapon is the breaking point as it destroys the victim's trust and sense of safety.

The help of legal and domestic violence professionals is invaluable as they are the people dedicated to guiding victims through the maze of custody, restraining orders, and all the other legal interventions that serve well to safeguard their loved ones. With the availability of proper tools and unshakeable faith in their own and family's well-being, the victims can embark on the journey of regaining their power and freeing their selves from the narcissist's influence.

Conclusion

The narcissist' playbook is a set of strategies that are a devastating and scary collection of manipulation techniques; these techniques are designed to relentlessly disintegrate the victim's sense of self, independence, and connection to the outside world. From the smooth engineering of hoovering and love-bombing to the latter's explosive psychological effects, which could disorient and dishearten even the most 'strong-willed individual,' the narcissist's vast collection of manipulative habits can make a victim feel stuck and powerless.

However, one should not forget that the tactics of the narcissist, which are indeed devastating, do not necessarily mean that the victim's value and character are flawed. What marks the narcissist is the endless desire to control, to be validated, and to have their needs elevated above anything else. Seeing through the manipulation is the most important thing: the narcissist tries by all means to save his false self-conscious superior mind. This step is a substantial part of the healing and recovery process.

By arming themselves with information, forming a robust support system, and making active steps in shielding their physical, psychological, and financial health, victims can commence a process of regaining control consequently paving a traumatizing life. Through the intervention from mental health professionals, legal experts, and fellow sufferers, the path back to the true self from the clutches of Narcissistic abuse would be a challenge but a battle worth winning with the promise of new horizons, strength, and freedom.

As this chapter comes to a close, we leave with the knowledge and strength, knowing that the narcissist's worst notwithstanding, our resilience, our courage, and the determination to free ourselves and our lives will always triumph. By doing so, we not only free ourselves, but we also encourage others to do the same and consequently achieve the goal of a world where the psychopath is buried deep in history, never again threatening our peace and safety.

Part II: Identifying and Addressing the Damage

You see, in the last chapters, we have drilled into the arsenal of cold-hearted manipulation strategies used by the narcissist for the sole purpose of undermining the victim's self-esteem, independence, and worldview. From the subtle manipulation of love-bombing and hoovering to the destructive consequence of economic abuse and making loved ones weapons, the narcissist's behaviors can leave their victims totally under their thumb, bewildered, and disempowered.

Still, the damage done by narcissistic abuse is not due merely to the obvious acts of the narcissist but also to the deep and long-lasting mental scars that he leaves behind. Repeated disregard, devaluing, and manipulation of a victim can lead to deep trauma which, in turn, impacts negatively their self-esteem, emotional health, and their ability to trust their self-perception and memory.

The deeper the victim gets into the trap of a narcissist's manipulation, the more they may doubt themselves, their perceived sanity, and their worth as they start realizing they are in a battle fighting alone. Trauma bonds that are established as a consequence of the manipulative conduct of the narcissist complicate the situation leading to the inability to escape the circle of hopelessness and despair.

It is within this treacherous setting that a healing journey, as well as recovery of the broken road, should start. In part II of this handbook, we will go deeper into the narcissistic abuse world, talking about how the victim's identity core is undermined and the steps they can take to rebuild their power as well as their truth.

Through gaining a deeper grasp of the psychological and emotional destruction by narcissistic abuse, readers will acquire the resources and the knowledge needed to unravel the tangles of gaslighting and emotional manipulation, heal the wounds of devaluation and betrayal, and start the process of mending of the shattered self-esteem.

This section will be a beacon for those who have been engulfed in the darkness of narcissistic abuse, guiding the journey of self-acceptance, self-compassion, and rejuvenation of their real selves. Through the implementation of the points listed earlier, victims can become aware of the differences between themselves and the narcissist, and they can regain their intrinsic positive qualities.

As the journey ahead may not be an easy one, with adequate support, resources, and a determination to their healing, they can rise out of the ashes of their trauma, stronger, more knowledgeable, and more empowered than before. It is high time that narcissists free themselves from the narcissist's influence and take hold of the unlimited resources they possess.

Chapter 4: Unraveling the Web of Gaslighting and Emotional Abuse

As we proceed further into the horrifying effects of narcissistic abuse, a particularly vicious and devastating strategy is used by narcissists: the craft of gaslighting. This manipulation is defined as a methodical destruction of the victim's reality, making the victim doubt their memories, perceptions, and judgment. The narcissist pours out the rain of lies, misinterpretations, and contradictions, as a result of which an individual becomes more and more unstable, and confused about themselves.

Understanding the Mechanisms of Gaslighting

Gaslighting often starts with seemingly harmless little events. The narcissist will be deemed not to have made a particular statement or promise, even when there is a clear recollection of it by the victim. They will possibly label the victim as "memory-faulty" or "overreacting," leaving the victim confused about their own experiences. Gradually this pattern snowballs, with the narcissist rewriting the story over and over again to fit their agendas.

In such extreme situations, the narcissist might deny the events that happened in the presence of the victim. They may say that the victim is "making it up" or "imagining it," in which case the victim is robbed of their truth and led to question their sanity instead. This can be utterly confusing and devastating so the victim feels more and more lonely and unworthy of trusting themselves.

The processes underpinning this type of emotional abuse are not only intricate but also sinister and manifold. The narcissist is continually contemptuous of the victim's views and experiences, thus setting up the predator in a position of dominance and control. As a result, the victim becomes dependent on the narcissist's version of reality. This, in the end, destroys the victim's inner confidence and self-esteem, making them more and more susceptible to the narcissist's manipulations.

Recognizing the Signs of Emotional Manipulation

One of the first steps in unraveling the web of gaslighting and emotional abuse is to develop a keen awareness of the subtle and not-so-subtle signs that something is amiss. This can include, but is not limited to:

- Frequent contradictions and denials of past events or statements

- Dismissive or belittling responses to the victim's thoughts, feelings, and concerns

- Accusations of "overreacting" or being "too sensitive" when the victim expresses emotion

- Persistent efforts to sow doubt and confusion in the victim's mind

- Shifting blame and responsibility for the narcissist's actions

- Discrediting the victim's memories or experiences as "imagined" or "false"

It is important to note that these tactics are not always overt or immediately recognizable. Narcissists are often skilled at masking their abusive behaviors behind a veneer of charm, rationality, and even concern for the victim's well-being. The key is to pay attention to patterns of behavior, rather than isolated incidents, and to trust one's instincts when something feels off.

The Erosion of Self-Trust and Self-Worth

As more and more time the victim spends on the narcissist's trapping of gaslighting and emotional manipulation, they will eventually feel the erosion of self-trust and self-worth very deeply. Their senses being constantly invalidated can cause profound confusion, disorientation, and the emergence of an opinion that they are "crazy" or "broken" at their core.

This loss of self-confidence can result in various long-term effects including difficulties in decision-making, trusting one's judgment, and one's personal needs and boundaries. So, they may become more and more dependent on approval and validation from the narcissist, and even reluctant to voice their own opinions in fear of the narcissist's consequences.

The effect on the self-worth of the victim is also the same. As the abuser's crushing attitude and ignoring the victim's thoughts, feelings, and experiences become more and more cruel, the victim may think that she/he is worthless, unlovable, and undeserving of even minimal attention and respect.

Erosion of self-confidence can be demonstrated in various ways ranging from chronic self-doubt and feelings of inadequacy to a profound sense of guilt, shame, and even a total identity loss. The victim might feel unable to find their strengths, individual talents, or inherent worth because they have been conditioned to believe that their value is always dependent on the narcissist's fickle approval.

Dealing with Chronic Invalidation and Devaluation

Unique to narcissistic emotional abuse is the persistent invalidation and devaluation of a victim's thoughts, opinions, and experiences. The narcissist may denigrate, minimize or even generally deny the veracity of the victim's feelings and call them "overreactions", "irrational" or "unwarranted".

The long-term invalidation can be very destructive, as it gradually leads to the victim having less sense of self and distrusting their intuition or feelings. Over time, the victim is likely to eventually rationalize their reactions and behaviors, always doubting their needs or boundaries, and ultimately depending on the narcissist's approval and validation.

Devaluation, conversely, is associated with narcissists' intentional devaluation of the victim's self-esteem, competence, and skills. It can be expressed as continuous criticism, arrogant statements, and outright contempt that will reduce the self-worth and self-confidence of the victim.

People who are being devalued constantly wrestle with symptoms of low self-esteem, self-doubt, and worthlessness. They could be frequenting the narcissist trying to prove themselves and their value, and only arousing further rejections and dismissals.

Overcoming the damaging effects of chronic invalidation and devaluation requires a multifaceted approach, involving both internal and external resources. This may include:

- Engaging in self-compassion and self-affirmation exercises to counter the narcissist's distorted messaging

- Seeking the support of trusted friends, family members, or mental health professionals who can validate the victim's experiences

- Challenging the narcissist's narrative by reclaiming one's own truth and personal history

- Gradually rebuilding self-trust and self-worth through conscious, intentional self-care and personal growth

Overcoming the Cognitive Dissonance

One of the most difficult and puzzling parts of dealing with the aftermath of gaslighting and emotional abuse is the cognitive dissonance that comes with it. This inner conflict between the real victim's lived experiences and the narcissist's twisted version of reality may be extremely puzzling and bewildering, causing the victim to feel that she or he is stuck in a state of perpetual confusion and self-doubt.

The narcissist's ability to skillfully manipulate emotions and the victim's deep-rooted desire to maintain the relationship and hold onto the idealized version of the narcissist are usually two significant factors that help to amplify the cognitive dissonance experienced by victims of narcissistic abuse. Despite the overwhelming proof of the narcissist's abusive behaviors, the victim may hang on to the idea that the narcissist is just "not that bad" or they still can "fix" the relationship.

It can be a constant struggle and emotional drain for the victim as they struggle to come to terms with the differences between the narcissist's public image and the private reality of the abusive relationship. The fear of being told they are "crazy" or "overreacting" can aggravate the victim's lack of trust in their intuition, creating a constant state of self-questioning and confusion.

Overcoming cognitive dissonance requires a multifaceted approach that encompasses both emotional and cognitive strategies. This may involve:

- Engaging in a process of reality-testing, where the victim carefully examines the evidence of the narcissist's abusive behaviors and the impact on their well-being

- Seeking the support of trusted friends, family members, or mental health professionals who can provide an objective, outside perspective

- Practicing self-compassion and challenging the internalized belief that the victim is "at fault" for the abuse

- Gradually building the courage and self-trust to assert one's reality, even in the face of the narcissist's denials and gaslighting

By persistently and patiently chipping away at the cognitive dissonance, the victim can begin to reclaim their sense of reality, self-worth, and the confidence to take the necessary steps towards healing and recovery.

Breaking Free from the Cycle of Self-Doubt

Victims of gaslighting and emotional abuse often confront a never-ending cycle of self-doubt and cognitive dissonance that is one of the most difficult things to deal with. Caught in the snare of doubt and confusion, they may lose even the ability to trust their judgment and make the right decisions, to save themselves and to get back on track.

To go beyond this cycle, the determination to embark on a self-discovery mission, self-acceptance, and trust-building are the pillars. Thus, the course usually begins with the victim realizing that shame and self-blame are not their inherent features but rather the result of the narcissistic wounding that the perpetrator inflicts on the victim through manipulation.

By way of counseling, therapy, and the strong support of trusted friends, victims can begin challenging the deep-rooted ideas of low self-esteem and inadequacy. They may learn to recognize the patterns of gaslighting and devaluation of emotions as well as to actively refuse to exchange their narcissist's distorted reality for their own 'lived experiences'.

Then the process of discovering one's truth and, in consequence, it is empowering and even extremely challenging. Victims may experience a counter-reaction, denial, and even abuse escalation from a narcissist whenever they try to resist their control. Nevertheless, if the victims hold fast to their conviction of themselves and they can trust their judgment, they can slowly but surely wiggle their way out of the cycle of self-doubt and again reclaim their autonomy, their self-worth, and their right to define their reality.

It should be understood that the trip is not a linear one and that the victim may experience setbacks and waves of doubt on the way. The road to recovery is paved with patience, self-care, and a strong conviction that one's worth and resilience are intrinsic. Adequate assistance, materials, and total devotion to themselves during their healing process can eventually help victims of gaslighting and emotional abuse to get out of the darkness, tougher, wiser, and more empowered.

Chapter 5: Healing the Wounds of Devaluation and Betrayal

Through these previous chapters, we reviewed that the narcissists' exhaustive devaluation, invalidating, and betraying of their victims' souls may result in permanent scars on the mind. The cognitive deconstruction of confidence, the shattering of trust, and the sensitively numb feeling of disorientation and loss that accompany the termination of a narcissistic relationship can be completely overpowering and incapacitating.

Hereinafter, we investigate the process of overcoming the harms caused by the narcissist's devaluation and betrayal. We will scrutinize the complicated process of grieving that victims must go through, unravel the trauma bonds that have been violently keeping them enslaved, and walk through the difficult path of rebuilding self-esteem and self-trust in the aftermath of such dramatic invalidation and dismissal of their very being.

Grieving the Loss of the Idealized Relationship

The painful part of the process of healing from narcissistic abuse is the stage involving the grieving of the idealized relationship that the victim had devoted so much energy to. The first part of the relationship with the narcissist when they are love bombing the victim with extreme affection and displays of love, can make the victim think that they are in a fairy-tale romance, they might want to believe that they are going to have a happy ever after with the narcissist.

Initially, the victim falls for the narcissist's charm, but as the relationship develops and his real self starts coming out, the victim realizes that the romance she thought she had was, in fact, a cleverly maneuvered facade – a fake paradise designed to attend to the narcissist's own needs and not to form a freely shared relationship.

This revelation is a very painful experience as the victim not only grieves the loss of their partner but also the loss of the imaginary self that has been created by the narcissist's support. The loss of the relationship may make the victim mourn the future they dreamt, the dreams that they invested in, and the sense of belonging and belongingness that the loved one was once a source of.

The victim's journey of mourning is a process fraught with many intricate emotions including anger, hatred, profound sadness, and utter sense of betrayal. Victims are called to recognize and approve of these emotions instead of trying to deny or suppress them which is the starting of the way to healing.

Unpacking the Trauma Bonds and Dependence

Along with the grieving process, one has to deal with the trauma bonds and emotional entanglement that has happened as a result of the narcissist's manipulative actions. These trauma bonds, formed in the course of a narcissist's wave of idealization, devaluation, and occasional display of affection, can be an incredibly powerful and disturbing type of attachment that is very difficult to get away from.

An emotional and psychological dependence of the victim on the narcissist's approval and confirmation can be very deep and may originate from the gradual depletion of the victim's self-value and autonomy by the narcissist. As the victim's concept of self-identity became more and more entwined with the narcissist's skewed view of them, the victim may have abandoned the ability to define their worth and purpose apart from the narcissist's relationship.

Working through these trauma links and regaining inner independence is a hard and emotionally exhausting process. It will probably include overcoming the ingrained fear of rejection, the omnipresent need for the narcissist's recognition, and the intrinsic sense of self-worthlessness, that the victim developed during taking the abuse.

Through counseling, therapy, and a strong network of confidants, the target of the narcissist can start to fight the cognitive distortions and fabricated narratives that have been inflicted on them. They will be taught what independence means, both in terms of self-value and autonomy to live their own life uncontrolled by the narcissist.

Addressing Feelings of Shame, Guilt, and Unworthiness

One of the most subtle and holistic impacts of narcissistic abuse is the victim's internalization of the narcissist's distorted perceptions and the corresponding feeling of shame, guilt, and low self-esteem. The continuous disqualification, disownment, and attack from a narcissist can make the victim think that they are worthless, unlovable, and don't deserve respect or basic human rights.

These feelings of shame and unworthiness may be so pervasive and difficult to master because they become part of the victim's view of self-value and their self-identity. The victim is likely to lose their self-worth and be unable to recognize their strengths and qualities. This is because they were always taught that their value is only dependent on the narcissist's changing validation and approval.

Facing these subconscious feelings of shame and worthlessness is an important part of the healing process. This could be done through self-compassion exercises, challenging internalized negative thoughts and ultimately building healthy self-esteem and self-confidence.

Through the introduction of counseling, support groups, and a trusted network of friends, victims have an opportunity to reevaluate the situation and realize that the shame and guilt they have been carrying should not be perceived as belonging to them but as a result of the narcissist's deceitful strategies.

Navigating the Aftermath of Devaluation and Discard

Once the victim starts removing themselves from the narcissist's web of control and manipulation, they might then have to deal with the effects of the narcissist devaluing and discarding them. The abrupt transition from being the main focus of the narcissist's love and attention to suddenly being discarded and treated like a worthless object can be very confusing and extremely painful.

The victim may go through a wide spectrum of emotions from unimaginable sadness and grief to extreme enraging and profound betrayal. It is often the case that they begin doubting themselves and their worth, especially trying to understand what they did wrong to deserve such treatment from the narcissist.

This transitional period can be extra stressful, as the victim tries to come to terms with the loss of the relationship, the shattered illusions, and the arduous task of rebuilding her/his life and sense of self after the narcissist has left their life.

Victims must understand that what has happened to them is not a result of self-depreciation, but rather a part of the narcissist's manipulative act to keep control and seek a narcissistic supply.

Through the assistance of counseling, support groups, and a core team of faithful allies, victims can be able to reconstruct the motives and actions of the narcissist, and at the same time regain their sense of worth and value, outside of the warped ideas of the narcissist.

Rebuilding Self-Esteem and Self-Trust

Perhaps one of the most daunting and crucial aspects of the healing journey for victims of narcissistic abuse is the process of rebuilding their shattered self-esteem and self-trust. The relentless devaluation, invalidation, and betrayal experienced at the hands of the narcissist can leave deep scars on the victim's psyche, eroding their confidence, self-worth, and belief in their capabilities and worthiness.

Reclaiming a healthy, positive sense of self-esteem and self-trust is essential for the victim to break free from the narcissist's grip and forge a fulfilling, authentic life beyond the confines of the abusive relationship. This process may involve a multifaceted approach, including:

- Engaging in self-affirmation exercises to challenge the internalized negative beliefs

- Seeking the support of counselors, therapists, and support groups to unpack the trauma and rebuild self-worth

- Gradually expanding one's social network and engaging in activities that foster a sense of purpose and accomplishment

- Practicing self-care, self-compassion, and mindfulness to nurture the wounded inner self

- Celebrating small victories and acknowledging personal growth and progress along the way

It is important to note that rebuilding self-esteem and self-trust is not a linear process and that the victim may experience setbacks and moments of doubt throughout their healing journey. Patience, self-compassion, and a steadfast commitment to their well-being will be crucial as they navigate this challenging terrain.

Letting Go of the Need for Closure or "Justice"

The closure or a sense of justice being coveted by many victims of narcissistic abuse can become a powerful force in their healing path. The desire to comprehend the reason behind narcissists' abusive behavior, to challenge them, or to see them becoming answerable for their actions may be a powerful impulse.

Nevertheless, understanding that the desire to get closure or "justice" about narcissistic abuse is commonly an illusionary goal is highly recommended. A narcissistic person is a person who is inherently averse to self-reflection, accountability, and change. Probably they will go further with denying, deflecting, and blaming the victim rather than showing remorse and validation the victim wants to see.

The fact that narcissists will never acknowledge or take responsibility for the damage they have caused may make letting go of the desire for closure or "justice" even more challenging and painful. This requires facing reality and the harsh reality that the narcissist never is going to acknowledge or take responsibility for the pain they have caused. This recognition may cause the individual to become frightened and make a renewed wave of mourning, anger, and dissatisfaction arise.

Despite this, the victim will realize that his healing and growth do not depend on the narcissist's recognition or regret. By breaking the victim's focus on the narcissist and placing it on their own self-empowerment and personal transformation, the victims begin to take back their power and move forward with the message of purpose and firmness.

This might entail embracing therapeutic methods to facilitate acceptance, forgiveness (of oneself and others), and a change in point of view – not towards the narcissist, but towards the victim's own natural value, power, and ability to grow and heal.

Eventually, the journey of giving up on looking for "closure" or "justice" is something highly personal and a victim must be kind and gentle with himself/herself in facing the challenges of this path. The right partnership of support, resources, and an unwavering dedication to self-care can help the victims find a way that will let them step out of being controlled by the narcissist's words and actions and go on with their future filled with chances and joys.

Chapter 6: Restoring Your Self-Esteem After Constant Invalidation

In the preceding chapters, we discovered that the perpetual disparagement, condemnation, and emotional invalidation that are endemic to narcissistic abuse can have a dreadfully deleterious effect on the victim's identity and ego. The unstoppable communication by the narcissist that the survivor is "not good enough," is "unworthy," or "has flaws" can be internalized too deeply by the victim who struggles to see their own as the base.

This chapter will go into detail about the process of rebuilding and restoring your self-esteem after narcissistic abuse. We will look at how these distortions have influenced your perception of self and learn ways to challenge the negative self-talk, build self-compassion, and develop a self-worth that is independent of the narcissist's judgment.

The Impact of Narcissistic Abuse on Self-Perception

One of the most resounding and lasting effects of narcissistic abuse is that it can significantly change the personalities of the victims and how they see themselves. The unremitting disrespect, defiance, and discreditation that the victim goes through at the hands of the narcissist may slowly erode the confidence, trustworthiness, and self-esteem of the victim.

Along with the narcissist's warped views and perspectives, the victim may increasingly be bombarded by a sinking feeling that he or she is in reality "unworthy," "flawed," or "unlovable" – a toxic discourse that may prove to be devastating for their emotional, mental, and physical being.

Self-esteem can ultimately be seen in a range of ways such as chronic self-doubt even a state of inferiority and finally complete loss of confidence in one's own judging abilities and decision-making skills. The victim may end up questioning everything he or she thinks or does, always afraid of the narcissist's judgment or critique.

On another hand, the victim's self-esteem can be tied so intricately to the narcissist's warped assessment that they might find it hard to remember what their own real strengths, special skills, and main values are. A narcissist´s constant picking on the target´s flaws and weaknesses can become the leading narrative, thus the victim's true self and capabilities are drowned out by this narrative.

Recognizing and Challenging Negative Self-Talk

A vital measure in reestablishing your self-worth after suffering from narcissistic abuse is to identify the negative self-talk and internalized beliefs of the narcissist through their repeated invalidation and devaluation of you. This is because these long-established patterns of self-criticism, self-doubt, and self-loathing are sneaky and widespread, and they can stand in the way of your recovery and success.

It is crucial to accept the fact that this type of negative self-talk is not a manifestation of your true worth or capabilities but a narcissist's means of manipulating you. The derogatory abuses, the demeaning taunts, and the constant belittling of your self-esteem have become now ingrained in your mind, and it is your job to untangle and unlearn these destructive thought patterns.

One useful tactic is that of self-reflection and self-monitoring. Every time you start negatively talking to yourself – whether you say something to yourself that you consider a mistake, you doubt your abilities, or you criticize your appearance – just stop and think about where these thoughts are coming from. Say to yourself, "Is this my voice, or the voice of the narcissist who keeps playing in my mind?"

As your awareness grows, you can then actively challenge and rephrase these negative thoughts. Balance each negative thought with a more realistic and compassionate one. Keep in mind your strong points, your great successes, and that you have a unique value in yourself, which should not be influenced by the narcissist's wrong assessment of you.

It is about a deliberate self-reflective and self-correcting thought process that often is very empowering as it allows you to reclaim your agency and assert your story against the narcissist's constant invalidation. Using practice and perseverance, you will step by step overcome the critical self-talk by replacing it with positive self-talk that will help you with the rebuilding of your damaged self-esteem.

Developing Self-Compassion and Self-Acceptance

Together with the procedure of questioning negative self-talk, it is very important to develop self-compassion and accept yourself to rebuild your self-esteem from narcissistic abuse. The continuous criticizing, undervaluing, and emotional denial by the narcissist probably made you feel

greatly ashamed, guilty, and undeserving of love or respect –
not only from others but also from yourself.

Forming a position of self-compassion is to understand that
you are a human, who should receive kindness, empathy, and
comprehension - especially when it comes to your own
perceived flaws or deficiencies. It implies recognizing the
pain and suffering you have gone through and showing
yourself the same warmth of understanding as what you
would give to a close friend or family member.

Accepting oneself means acknowledging and welcoming all
parts of you - the good, the bad, the unique traits, and even
vulnerabilities - with an attitude of receptiveness, interest,
and total positive evaluation. It's also understanding that your
value doesn't depend on how narcissists see or accept you but
it's something inside yourself that cannot be taken away from
who you are as a person.

Doing certain activities like self-affirmation, mindfulness
meditation, and writing in a diary can greatly assist in the
development of self-compassion and self-acceptance. These
tools help you to actively respond against the negative
messages you have absorbed inside yourself, as well as to
intentionally grow a more caring and encouraging internal
talk.

Also, talking with a therapist or counselor who knows about
trauma-informed care can be very helpful. They know how
to guide you through the difficult emotional journey of
showing yourself compassion and accepting yourself. They
will give you methods and help that assist in restoring your
feeling of being valuable and self-love.

Always, the path toward self-compassion and self-acceptance
is not straight. There might be delays, times of uncertainty,

or even phases with strong emotional turbulence. Yet, through treating yourself gently, being patient, and focusing on your recovery, you can slowly construct the base of self-esteem that has been destroyed by the abuser's narcissism.

Redefining Your Worth Beyond the Narcissist's Opinion

A very deep and tough job in rebuilding your self-esteem from narcissistic abuse is finding new definitions for your worth that are separate from what the narcissist wrongly perceives, judges, or devalues. The constant attention of a narcissist on what they see as your "imperfections" and "inadequacies" might have made this the main way you started to see yourself, leaving feelings of being stuck in a story not created by you alone.

Recovering your inner worth and value requires a basic change in how you see yourself – moving away from seeing yourself as the narcissist does, towards re-establishing a connection with your genuine self, values that are important to you, and natural abilities or skills. This procedure needs self-examination, finding oneself again, and being ready to question the restricted thoughts and stories placed on you by the narcissist.

Start with a self-examination, writing in your journal, and thinking deeply. Look into the parts of yourself that you truly cherish, like qualities, abilities, and characteristics that are independent from narcissist's opinions or approval. What gives you happiness, satisfaction, and a feeling of having meaning? What are the unique attributes that make you who you are?

While you explore these parts of your true self, try to increase and enjoy them more. Get involved in activities and interests that match your hobbies and beliefs. Also, connect with people who understand and value you for the real person that you are. Little by little, this will help in forming a renewed feeling of self-esteem based on your encounters, not the twisted viewpoints of narcissism.

We understand this procedure to redefine your worth is not simple. Probably, the narcissist's impact has become deeply rooted, and reversing their harm can be a slow and tough path. But if you have patience with yourself, show self-kindness, and keep dedicating to healing plus personal development; then you can regain strength and assert your intrinsic value regardless of what the narcissist thinks.

Reclaiming Your Autonomy and Decision-Making Power

Very closely connected to getting back your self-esteem is the regaining of your ability to make decisions and be independent – two key qualities that the abuser has purposefully taken from you during the abusive relationship.

One of the key features of narcissistic abuse involves the unyielding attempt of the narcissist to take and keep complete control and dominance over the victim. This can take different forms, from financial control and resource manipulation to degradation of the victim's choice and self-trust.

As narcissists more and more penetrate your system, you may start depending more and more on its approval, guidance, and permission even for daily matters. Such removal of freedom can be deeply emasculating, making you feel enslaved, unable to defend yourself, and almost completely subject to whatever the narcissist will do.

Gaining back that power of decisions is a vital step in the recovery of your self-esteem. It is all about consciously rejecting the narratives and beliefs that have kept you in the narcissist's control and actively choosing to make choices that align with your values, needs, and desires.

The process that may be adopted is essentially a step up from independent decision-making, which starts with small, meaningless decisions and gradually moves to larger and more consequential ones. Along with this, it may also include reaching out to pals, relatives, or experts who can give an outside perspective and cheerleading as one navigates the unknown roads.

Along with regaining your decision-making authority, you should also focus on restoring your self-trust in your instincts, judgments, and choices as the fundamentals of your life. This may involve actively fighting the self-doubt and questions that the narcissist has put there, as well as proactively verifying that you at least have the right to make decisions for your benefit.

With each small step you take towards regaining a sense of control over your life and your choices, you will move closer to a profound change in the way you view yourself and measure yourself. You no longer have to suffer under a narcissist's aggressive demands and unrealistic expectations, but instead, realize that you write your narrative and steer your vessel.

Embracing Your Authentic Strengths and Qualities

The last step, which can be truly freeing, is when you accept and appreciate your real strengths, talents, and qualities. These are the things about yourself that the narcissist kept attacking and making less important.

Now, as you sail through the hard path of fighting negative self-talk, nurturing self-compassion, and taking back your independence, probably you are starting to discover all the different special things that form who you truly are. These could be traits that the narcissist has ignored or degraded; they might also represent parts of yourself that have become distant due to turbulence in an abusive bond.

No matter where they come from, it's time to make these natural strengths and abilities visible - not just acknowledge them but also appreciate their existence. Let these qualities be the base as you construct a fresh understanding of your values and self-confidence.

This could mean doing things and chasing interests that help you rediscover your natural abilities and loves, such as expressing art, investigating intellectually, or showing physical skill. It might also include looking for approval and confirmation from dear ones who are trustworthy - they can reflect the exceptional characteristics they notice in you.

The most essential thing is a strong dedication to respect and acceptance of your true self, with no need for excuses or holding back. This means releasing the restricting ideas and uncertain feelings about yourself that a narcissistic person has put in you. Instead, develop a powerful and unapologetic love towards who you are.

While you embrace and accept your strong points along with distinctive traits, there will be a deep change in how you see yourself and feel powerful. You are not limited by the wrong views of narcissists anymore; instead, you can take back your place in this world - one that is full of value, strength, and endless possibilities.

This adventure of finding oneself again and accepting oneself is not simple. There could be obstacles and setbacks during the process. However, if you have patience, show kindness to yourself, and stay dedicated to your healing and development, then you can come out from the ruins left by narcissistic abuse stronger in strength yet more understanding while also feeling closer to what makes up "you".

Part III: Charting Your Path to Recovery

At this turning point in your process of healing and taking back yourself, it's crucial to acknowledge the big advancement you have already achieved. The initial two segments of this book are about expanding your comprehension of narcissistic abuse, untying the intricate manipulation and emotional destruction, as well as preparing for deep interior labor that is yet to come.

You met head-on with the narcissist's twisted views and how they corroded your self-image. You started the tough task of regaining self-worth, taking back who you truly are, and growing in self-kindness even when constantly invalidated. These are not easy achievements, so appreciate the bravery, strength, and persistence that brought you here.

Now, standing at the doorway of Part III, it is time to turn your attention towards mapping out the route for complete healing and freedom. This section in the book will steer you through important stages: detaching yourself from trauma connections that have tied you down with narcissists, making firm limits for your safety, and developing skills plus tactics needed to regain control of life on personal conditions.

The way ahead is not simple. There will be times of extreme sorrow, fury, and uncertainty as you face the deeply rooted habits of thinking and acting that a narcissist has put in your mind. But as you continue to move forward, each time will see a gradual recovery - regaining strength, independence, and the ability to live without any control from narcissists.

In the next sections, you will acquire skills to cut off the emotional connections that have kept you tied to abuse. You will also learn how to establish and make sure boundaries are respected for safeguarding your physical, emotional, and digital health. Additionally, find out methods for nurturing self-compassion and strength needed to endure the difficulties in the healing process.

Crucially, you will also learn about methods for managing the intricate grieving phase that usually comes with losing an idealized relationship. You'll study ways to achieve closure and tranquility, even if the narcissist does not provide validation or responsibility.

When you start this changing part of your life, keep in mind that you are not the only one doing it. Many people have gone on this journey before and the group knowledge and help from those in recovery is there to guide and strengthen you. Believe in yourself - believe that you can grow, become better, and decide on your healing path. Understand that every step ahead helps bring back the life that was always yours to claim back.

Chapter 7: Breaking the Trauma Bonds: Letting Go of the Narcissist's Grip

As we have already learned in the previous chapters, the terrible effects of narcissistic abuse reach deeper than the fact that narcissist directly displays pernicious behavior. The most riotous and profoundly down-to-the-bone consequence of that profound kind of emotional and mental abuse is the trauma bond which is a strong and unsettling emotional attachment that can make victims feel inexplicably drawn to their abuser even after the relationship has ended.

This chapter will explore the complicated dynamics of trauma bonds by analyzing the underlying mechanisms and the coping strategies that victims can use to realize and manage them. We will, among other things, have to consider the terrible fear of being abandoned and rejected that drives the trauma bond creation, and understand how the delicate process of putting up boundaries is important in breaking the narcissist's grip.

Understanding the Psychology of Trauma Bonds

The basis of trauma bonding is a very complex mix of human psychology, neurochemistry, and the narcissist's manipulations. When the targeted individual feels intermittent reinforcement with emotional highs and lows, as well as the constant threat of rejection or abandonment, the brain can be hardwired to crave the narcissist's attention and validation even in the presence of the narcissist's cruelty and abuse.

Here, the causes are associated with the brain's neurochemical systems that enable people to pursue and sustain close relationships with others. In a satisfying and mutual relationship, the release of feel-good neurotransmitters such as oxytocin and dopamine strengthens the connection between partners, which produces trust, security, and a sense of belonging.

Still, in the case of narcissistic abuse, these neurochemical pathways are used in a way that they consider the narcissist's sporadic emotional displays of attachment and affection as a source of unbelievable pleasure and relief. This fear of losing the perception of "connection" can motivate the victim to appease the narcissist further, irrespective of overwhelming proof of the narcissist's exploitative and controlling actions.

The additional layer of complexity that trauma bond embraces is a victim's sense of self-worth and identity which probably has already been undermined by a narcissist's unremitting assault of devaluation and emotional invalidation. The victim may feel overly attached to the narcissist, not only because of the neurochemical dependence but also because the narcissist has become the main source of the victim's sense of value and belonging – a state that makes the idea of letting go and moving on so distressing and associated with shyness.

Identifying and Severing the Emotional Attachments

Awareness and understanding of the emotional ties that are formed between the victim and the narcissist is the initial stage of escaping the claws of the trauma bond. Oftentimes the victim is forced to deal with the bitter truth that the 'love' he/she had for the narcissist was a carefully crafted delusion that was rooted in the narcissist's manipulative methods and the victim's desperation for validation and acceptance.

An acceptable way of identifying and uncovering these emotional ties is through the process of self-reflection and journaling in a structured manner. Through a detailed evaluation of the patterns of the relationship, the victim can start identifying exactly the particular moments, actions, or dynamics that have led to the creation of a trauma bond.

In this regard, the writer has talked about the beginning, where the narcissist used love bombing and idealizing to produce a sense of euphoric connection, followed by the later cycle of devaluation, abandonment, and intermittent affection which kept the victim in a state of perpetual emotional turmoil and dependence.

While the victim develops a thorough understanding of the psychological and emotional processes that create the trauma bond, the victim can proceed with a conscious breaking of these manipulative relationships. This might require doing tasks like questioning the narcissistic person's "love" or "cares," revealing the narcissistic person's true nature and goals, and painfully grieving the loss of the ideal relationship.

It is important to note that this process of severing emotional attachments is not a linear one and that the victim may experience setbacks, moments of doubt, and intense emotional upheaval along the way. The trauma bond has been deeply ingrained, and breaking free from its grip requires patience, self-compassion, and a steadfast commitment to the victim's healing and well-being.

Overcoming the Fear of Abandonment and Rejection

The most direct and crippling factors that can keep victims held in the bond of trauma are fear of abandonment and rejection or to be precise. The narcissist's constant belittling of the victim's self-esteem along with their occasional displays of warmth and withdrawals can induce a psychologically numbing fear of being cast away and exposed.

The fear of abandonment could be demonstrated in different ways; from placating the narcissist and keeping the relationship at all cost to a deeply rooted feeling that the victim is undeserving of love and belonging. The trauma bond works as a psychological prosthesis that has the victim drawn to the narcissist due to a need for acceptance and validation.

Addressing this fear of abandonment and rejection is the key element of the process of getting rid of the trauma bond. This is likely to be done through therapeutic interventions that get to the root of the victim's attachment difficulties, e.g., abusive or withholding parenting. This may mean developing a firm circle of trusted friends who could offer the victim the emotional resources and recognition that the narcissist has denied.

Furthermore, a victim may have to deal with the societal norms that may have been passed down by being constantly devalued and rejected by the narcissistic. This is a task that may be very difficult and very emotionally exhausting because the victim is looking at the conclusion that these judgments and opinions of narcissists are not a mirror of how much the victim is worth.

Self-compassion, affirmation, and the love of one's self are the instruments the victim can use to conquer the fear of abandonment and rejection and ultimately regain control and empowerment in the face of the narcissist's cruel manipulation.

Setting Boundaries and Enforcing Your Limits

The success of the victim in breaking the emotional ties and overcoming the paralyzing fear of solitude, which led to the trauma bond, hinges on the advocacy of healthy boundaries which is a key aspect of the healing process. The narcissist's persistent endeavors to assert authority over the victim will only be effectively countered through the clear, unshakeable enunciation of boundaries, which should be reinforced constantly.

This process of boundary-setting may involve a wide range of practical and emotional measures, such as:

- Maintaining strong personal, emotional, and cyber boundaries to provide the victim with space and confidentiality.
- Working on the abilities of being assertive and having the confidence to communicate one's needs and limits to the narcissist.
- Seeking the help of your faithful friends, family, or professionals to enforce and maintain these bounds.

- It makes sense to deprive or sever the bond between the narcissist and the victim, if needed, for the sake of the victim's emotional and mental health.
- Guarding one's financial resources and personal data from the narcissist's exploitative tactics.

At the most, the creation and execution of these rules are not one-time activities but rather ongoing processes that necessitate the victim's absolute persistence and vigilance. The narcissist will regularly test and try to break these limits using several different manipulative methods to regain their power and authority over the victim.

With continued persistence in defining boundaries, the victim will be able to gradually recover their independence and personal power, eventually breaking free from the narcissist's grasp and reclaiming their right to a life that is in no way influenced by the narcissist's negative behavior.

Navigating the Grieving Process and Finding Closure

A very difficult and emotionally draining part of breaking away from the trauma bond is the grieving process that the victim experiences during this period. The loss of the relationship, the disillusionment of the narcissist's real character, and the intense feelings of betrayal and sadness can result in a complex patchwork of feelings, including deep sadness, anger, confusion, and loss.

The victim needs to acknowledge and accept these feelings, and not try to bury them or ignore them. Loss of the ideal love and all the hopes and expectations that come with that is bound to elicit a natural and necessary response.

Using the help of counseling, support groups, and trusted friends/family, the victim gets the opportunity to face and let go of the most overwhelming feelings. One of these steps may be letting go by not sending letters to narcissists, rituals, or ceremonies to symbolize the end of the relationship, or even just giving yourself the space and time needed to feel the depth of your pain.

The significant aspect is that the grieving process is not necessarily linear and the victim may go through the various stages – denial, anger, bargaining, depression, and acceptance – several times before getting comfort and peace. This is a natural and expected part of the process of healing, and the victim needs to do it with compassion for self, patience, and the understanding that giving up on bad things is also hard and full of nuances.

While the victim is struggling with the process of grieving, he or she also may come across the need for closure or "justice" in the sense of the narcissist's inappropriate behavior. Although a desire for resolution, as well as an account from the narcissist, is understandable, the victim must understand that the search for closure from the narcissist is likely to be a fruitless endeavor.

By their character, narcissists are closed to personal introspection, being held accountable, and change. They hardly give up blaming victims, the denial and shifting the blame instead of providing them with the compassion they deserve. Leaving this behind and refusing to focus on the narcissist can be a deep and freeing experience that can help the victim turn away from the narcissist toward their healing and development.

Releasing the Need for the Narcissist's Validation

The last and probably the most important part of getting out of the bond is when the victim doesn't need the narcissist's validation and approval anymore. This strong reliance on the narcissist's view of the victim's value and self-worth has been at the root of the trauma bond. It is now time to detach the last, invisible rope that ties the victim to the abuser.

Through the cultivation of self-compassion, self-acceptance, and a growing feeling of self-worth, the victim gradually redirects their attention from the narcissist's distorted judgments to the value that they have within themselves that is independent of the narcissist. This is likely to be accompanied by doing activities that challenge the unconsciousness of the negative thinking and talking that the narcissist imposes, as well as developing more nurturing and affirmative inner dialogue.

As the victim recovers self-ownership and self-identification, they can acknowledge their value, their identity, and their belonging are not dependent on the narcissist's approval or validation. This powerful revelation may be emancipating and extremely distressing on the other hand, when the victim comes to terms with the problematic connections and attachments that have kept them in the narcissist's orbit forever.

The general release from the need for the narcissist's validation is not always a one-time event but is rather a process that takes patience, self-understanding, and a constant commitment to the victim's healing and growth. The victim may experience setbacks, moments of uncertainty, and the most painful of emotions as they struggle through this difficult journey.

However, by remaining vigilant, self-compassionate, and focused on their well-being, the victim can gradually sever the final threads of the trauma bond, reclaiming their power, their agency, and their rightful place in the world – a place where they are the sole arbiter of their worth and the authors of their destiny, free from the narcissist's influence and control.

Chapter 8: Setting Healthy Boundaries and Maintaining Your Protection

Establishing Physical, Emotional, and Digital Boundaries

Overcoming the crippling effects of narcissistic abuse involves first and foremost setting specific, unassailable boundaries. The boundaries are like the invisible but important lines that help determine your personal space, your emotional needs, and the level of access other people have to your life. Boundaries setting and enforcing is a vital part of the healing process for victims of emotional abuse by narcissists.

The physical boundaries include the limits you set around your physical space, your body, and your personal property. For example, the right to determine who can enter your home and what level of physical contact is comfortable can be added. Emotional boundaries are those limits that you put in place around your own emotions, thoughts, and energy. These could be, for instance, how much time and emotional work you are prepared to put into certain relationships, what topics are forbidden to be discussed, and how much vulnerability you can accept.

Digital boundaries are particularly relevant in the digital age being that our lives are becoming more technology driven. This may involve denying access to your social media account, limiting the kind of content you post online, and deciding what type of reaction to have regarding unsolicited messages or unwanted contact. Building firm digital boundaries will help you protect your privacy and avoid the narcissists to keep on meddling with your life by technological means.

Being specific, consistent, and unapologetic is what makes the difference in setting proper boundaries. Typically, you can easily violate unclear or inconsistently enforced frontiers. By establishing your boundaries clearly and confidently you are communicating to the world loudly and clearly that you are in charge of your own life and will not allow others to mistreat or take advantage of you.

Developing Assertiveness and Self-Advocacy Skills

While boundary-setting is crucial, it is also significant to learn to express and defend them correctly. Assertiveness, which means expressing your needs, feelings, and views in a direct but polite way, is a significant skill for narcissistic trauma survivors.

The narcissist is probably used to having you submissive, obedient, and not brave enough to stand up for yourself. Getting your assertiveness back means undoing those negative patterns and taking the courage to stand up for your voice. It can be frightening or unnatural at the beginning, but with time, you will get used to it.

Begin by figuring out your fundamental values, needs, and wants. What is worth to you? What are your non-negotiables? Knowing this foundation will simply make you assertive and self-confident.

Be sure to articulate your boundaries using "I" statements to show how you feel, rather than accusing "you" statements. For instance, "I get uncomfortable when you raise a loud voice at me" is better than "You need to stop shouting at me." It will not provoke a defensive reaction and will focus on you.

Be ready to reassert your boundary again firmly and unmoved even if the other person tries to argue, dismiss, or make you feel guilty. Narcissists frequently use different manipulation strategies to undermine your conviction, however, maintaining unflinching conviction is always the more effective long-term option.

Recollect that self-advocacy is all about being assertive and doing it in a way that shows respect for your needs. Initially, it might be challenging, but in time, this skill of advocating for yourself without hesitation will be an important part of your healing process.

Protecting Your Privacy and Personal Information

In the aftermath of narcissistic abuse, protecting your privacy and personal information is imperative. The narcissist has probably already broken your trust and crossed your boundaries with you, and may keep on using ways to get personal information about you or keep on controlling your life.

The first step is to do a survey on your digital footprint and do whatever you can to limit the amount of personal data available to you online. Review your social media privacy settings, consider deactivating any unused accounts, and think carefully about what you put out in public. Be careful of oversharing on social media, because the narcissist may use that information in their favor.

In addition, your physical privacy should be protected by careful screening of any new relationships or service providers who may have access to your home, properties, or important information. This could include stuff like house help, contractors, or even health workers. Rely on your gut feeling and don't shun seeking references or doing the required background check.

In the case the narcissist can get your finances under his control the way to go is to open a new bank account or credit card that he can't access. Regularly check out your accounts for any signs of misuse and put a credit freeze to prevent criminals from using your information.

Sometimes it is necessary to change your cell number, email address, or any other contact details to create a new clean break from the narcissist. Although this may seem like a hassle, it's well worth it for the security that it can bring.

Recall, you also possess the right to your privacy and the right to personal autonomy. Never ignore the needed action to protect your information and build boundaries that will keep you safe.

Dealing with the Narcissist's Attempts to Breach Boundaries

Despite all your attempts to establish and maintain healthy boundaries the narcissist either relentlessly or persistently tries to undermine them. This might be in the form of continuous calling, messaging, or even surprise visits to your house or workplace. They may attempt to manipulate your emotions, play the victim, or even use threats in a desperate attempt to break you.

Keep in mind that narcissistic behavior has nothing to do with you or the boundaries you have set, it is the self-centered nature, entitlement and disregard for yourself that is being exhibited. They are trying to make illegitimate incursions into your private space in a pathetic struggle to regain the control they lost over your life.

When handling these boundary-crossing behaviors, try not to encourage or respond emotionally to them. Rather than getting angry, just be assertive and consistent with your response. Unambiguously reiterate your boundary and the consequences for trespassing, for example, the termination of the conversation or reduced contact. If the narcissist keeps doing that, be ready to carry out those consequences, regardless of your emotions.

In certain scenarios, it might be necessary to take more severe legal action, such as filing a restraining order or a cease and desist letter. This is an intimidating adventure; hence, your security and health should come first. Talk to a lawyer or domestic violence advocate to know about your legal rights and available options.

Moreover, you should make sure you have a support network at hand to help you overcome difficult moments. Ask your close friends, relatives, or professionals, whoever can give emotional support, and practical assistance and keep you accountable to your boundaries.

Keeping your boundary lines in front of an insistent narcissist is exhausting, but it is a vital step to regaining the power and also your life. While it takes time, consistency, and endless determination, it is possible to overcome the narcissist's control and claim your right to be a self-determining individual.

Enlisting Support from Trusted Friends and Professionals

The process of recovery from narcissistic abuse is a deeply personal experience, but you don't have to go through it all by yourself. One of the ways to set and keep your healthy boundaries is by surrounding yourself with a network of people you trust and support you.

Begin with the individuals in your life who have never faltered in offering you sympathy, and support without any strings attached. Such people could be good friends, relatives, or colleagues who have seen the impact of Narcissistic abuse and are ready to listen, confirm your experience, and do some practical assistance for you.

Tell these reliable partners the reason you have boundaries and how they can help you to stick with them. This could range from straightforward activities, such as denying your contact with the narcissist or offering you a place to relax, to more complex ones, like accompanying you to critical meetings and events.

Besides your support network, give priority to professional services by therapists, counselors, and domestic violence advocates who are focused exclusively on narcissistic abuse. These are the individuals who can give you the most useful guide, tools, and resources to help you manage the complex process of instituting and maintaining boundaries.

An experienced therapist will assist you in checking the ones that have made you susceptible to boundary violations in the past. They can also collaborate with you in determining the right strategies for having your needs met, handling tough emotions, and growing resilience despite the narcissist's manipulations.

Domestic violence advocates provide specialized support like safety planning, legal assistance, and assistance in linking to community resources. They know what difficulties a victim of narcissistic abuse goes through and assist in defining what safety needs to be taken.

Remember, you don't have to face this journey alone. Surrounding yourself with a network of trusted allies - both personal and professional - can provide the emotional, practical, and moral support you need to reclaim your boundaries and your life.

Strategies for Setting and Enforcing Healthy Boundaries

Establishing and maintaining healthy boundaries is an ongoing process that requires a multifaceted approach. Here are some key strategies to consider as you work to set and enforce the boundaries you need:

1. Identify your boundaries: Begin by helping yourself determine your physical, emotional, and digital boundaries. What are your non-negotiables? What kind of behavior or situation will you not tolerate from now on? Be as distinct as you can.

2. Communicate your boundaries: First, identify where your boundaries are, then communicate them clearly and directly to the people in your life, including the

narcissist. Use "I" statements to specify how you feel and your needs rather than to make accusations or demands.

3. Set consequences: Concretely explain the outcomes due to the violation of your personal space, and be determined to do what you said without hesitation. This could be actions like finishing the conversation, reducing contact, or starting litigation.

4. Practice self-compassion: Maintaining and establishing boundaries can be difficult, and more so when you are dealing with the emotional manipulation and deceptions of a narcissist. Be self-compassionate during the journey and remember that your wellness and well-being are just as worthy of protection as anyone else's.

5. Build your support network: Have a confidante who will keep you accountable to your boundaries and be a source of support when that is needed most. They can be practical or emotional.

6. Document violations: Write down and maintain a detailed log of violations of boundaries, dates, times, and particular behaviors. This is paramount in case you decide to file a lawsuit or acquire additional professional guidance.

7. Seek professional help: Perhaps try working with a therapist or a domestic violence advocate who can assist you with creating effective boundary-setting methods and give advice on seeing out difficulties.

8. Prioritize self-care: Setting and keeping boundaries can be hard mentally and emotionally. Develop a

strategy of self-care techniques like meditation, exercise, and hobbies to help you maintain balance, and be refreshed along the way.

9. Be patient and persistent: The ability to set and stick to boundaries is something that we learn, and doing so can sometimes feel challenging, and takes some getting used to. Celebrate any progress, even if it's just marginal.

Keep in mind that keeping healthy boundaries is not all about being selfish or controlling; it is about respecting your needs, taking care of yourself, and restoring your sovereignty. Through sincerity and commitment, you can end up overcoming the bondage imposed by the narcissist and change your life into a safe and satisfying one.

Chapter 9: Cultivating Self-Compassion and Reclaiming Your Authentic Self

Reconnecting with Your Core Values and Beliefs

The aftermath of narcissistic abuse is by no means an easy time and, typically, one feels lost, and out of touch with the center of their being. The consistency of gaslighting, manipulation, and denial of reality brought about by the narcissist hurt one's self-perception, making it difficult to remember the identity you have always had such as your core values, beliefs, and aspirations.

The quest of rediscovering your authentic self goes hand in hand with the re-establishment of the core identity that the narcissist aimed to diminish or dominate. The process of this self-discovery can be very cleansing as you discover your true identity, which is free from a narcissist's skewed opinions and predictions about you.

Begin by spending some moments in silence where there is no chaos and interruptions like at home. Journal, meditate or do some other kind of introspective activities that will help you reflect on your subconscious thoughts and feelings. Consider questions such as: What is it that I value the most? What are the critical values that align with my choices and actions? Which ideas do I value most, and how have they contributed to my view of the world?

You may discover a lot of your own beliefs and values that were hidden or blurred by the narcissist's factors as you entered this process of self-discovery. Possibly at some point, you have highly valued the truth and integrity and the manipulation of the narcissist has caused you to question your moral code. Alternatively, could it be that you are an activist for social justice but the narcissist's selfishness confuses your dedication to the cause?

Reinforcing your authentic values and ideas will help you find your reason, way, and more so inner spirit. This revitalized sense of self will be kind of a north star for you in your journey of recovery as it will help you in sorting through the complexities of and in living a life that truly reflects your deepest beliefs.

Rediscovering Your Passions, Interests, and Aspirations

In addition to reconnecting with the principles and ideas you value the most, a vital part of the process involves rediscovering the things that give you life purpose and joy. The narcissist's desire to control and belittle your sense of self might have driven you to reject or disregard the very aspects of your life that make you pleased, ecstatic, and progressed as a person.

Set aside time to reminisce on the activities, hobbies, and interests that used to be the most meaningful and invigorating in your past. What were the activities that permitted you to get into the moment, to feel an enthralling feeling of flow and connection? What were the dreams and goals that you used to hold in your heart and believed in firmly until the narcissist's destructive influence started to eat away at your possibility?

It is crucial to put yourself in this process with patience and self-kindness. The narcissist might have got you convinced that your likes and dislikes are insignificant or unworthy of being considered. Defeat this psychological barrier by actively disputing those restricting beliefs and learning to grant yourself the freedom to try and experiment.

The first step is creating a list of the activities, topics, and endeavors that have always stirred up your curiosity, even if you haven't actively engaged in them for years. Give attention to digging into old hobbies, revisiting books or movies you have liked in the past, or exploring new experiences that make you excited. As you reconnect with these hobbies, focus on the feelings of joy, fulfillment, and satisfaction they make you experience.

Furthermore, apart from reviving your old fancies, try out completely different realms that you never dared to enter in your daily life. Adopt a beginner's mindset and be open to new ventures with the feeling of exciting exploration. You may always be surprised at what secret talents or undiscovered dreams you discover.

As you partake in the hobbies and enterprises that truly bring you happiness and meaning, you'll slowly rebuild the feeling of being in charge and self-determination. Your re-embracing the things you are passionate about will serve as a perfect antidote for the narcissist who tries to manipulate and lessen your self-esteem.

Embracing Your Unique Strengths and Capabilities

In addition to the rediscovery of your passions and aspirations, it is also equally important that you take a moment to celebrate your strengths and capabilities. You might find that the narcissist's constant devaluation and criticism leave you with an unstable belief in your abilities, where you regularly question or even disbelieve your worth and competence.

It is important to start by making a deliberate effort to shift from the narcissist's negative appraisals to a more reasonable and self-affirming standpoint. Take a deeper look into the list of life skills, talents, and virtues you have learned through narcissist manipulations and abuse.

Perhaps you have shown phenomenal resilience in the face of challenges and mastered the skill of empathizing intensely with other people. So, you might have a brilliant mind, which led you to success in your studies or career, or you're a creative genius that brings the world around us happiness and beauty.

Anyway, apart from the fact that you have specific abilities and talents, it's crucial to respect and celebrate yourself, and not through the narcissist's distorted viewpoint. Participate in frequent self-reflection activities that assist you to identify and acknowledge your invaluable and inherent value.

One amazing technique could be to generate a personal "brag book"- a journal or digital platform where you can store your achievements, accolades, and positive feedback from others. Reread this book when you have diminishing self-confidence, and keep it as a reminder of your true value in the physical form.

Moreover, make efforts to be in positions that reveal your strengths and capabilities. It can be just as fulfilling whether it is taking up a new project at work, volunteering for a cause you are passionate about, or engaging in activities that allow you to show your diverse talents so that you can feel empowered.

Keep in mind that the narcissist's incessant criticism and false devaluation don't mean it is who you are as a person. By recognizing and taking pride in the attributes, which make you unique you'll start reclaiming your self-value and self-assurance that will guide you to a more joyful life.

Nurturing Self-Compassion and Self-Acceptance

What is at the core of the process of rediscovering yourself is the creation of self-compassion and self-acceptance. Being the victim of a narcissist has probably caused you long-lasting pain, weakening your ability to care about yourself and how you take good care of other people.

Self-kindness is the act of giving yourself an equal measure of affection and warmth that you would bestow a dear friend or a loved one who is in pain. It is a process of seeing yourself as human, which includes accepting your weaknesses and defects and responding to your problems with care and love instead of harsh self-judgment.

For the victims of narcissistic abuse, self-compassion practice can be very tough. The narcissist has more often than not brainwashed you to have a perception of yourself as unworthy, unworthy of love, and inadequate. To eliminate the deeply rooted cycle of self-hatred, you should engage in this deliberate, ongoing practice of rephrasing your inner dialogue.

Start by noticing carefully what you say to yourself – the continuous flow of thoughts and evaluations that occur in your mind. When you catch yourself engaging in harsh self-criticism, pause and ask yourself: "Would I talk to my dear friend in the same way?" If your answer is no, stop that and start filling your head with kinder, more understanding thoughts instead.

Keep in mind that you are a human being and that being in pain, going through struggles, and facing challenges is just a part of being a human being. Instead of scolding yourself for your perceived faults or errors, try to affirm yourself with the same kindness and empathy as you would do with your loved ones if they did it.

As well as being kind to oneself, it is really important to know how to accept oneself too. The process entails accepting who you are: your strengths and weaknesses, the distinct characteristics and habits that make you uniquely you, incorporating your past and present into a whole, with having to reject any parts that do not fit.

Self-acceptance doesn't imply that you are settling for remaining the same; instead, it's about getting a basis of unconditional self-loving and respect and growing/evolving from a position of inner peace and the realization of your potential.

To establish self-acceptance, you may try positive self-talk, self-reflection exercises, and mindfulness meditation, for example. Do not need to prove yourself all the time or to be something to satisfy other people's demands.

Recall that the development of self-compassion and self-acceptance is a continuous one, a process that entails patience, persistence as well as the willingness to challenge the entrenched norms of self-criticism and self-doubt. By taking each step, you'll be reinvented into the real version of yourself, the basis for a better and happier existence.

Letting Go of the Narcissist's Distorted Perceptions

One of the most significant challenges in reclaiming your authentic self after narcissistic abuse is the need to let go of the narcissist's deeply ingrained, distorted perceptions of who you are. The narcissist has likely projected their insecurities, biases, and warped sense of reality onto you, leaving you struggling to see yourself.

Throughout the abusive relationship, the narcissist may have constantly criticized, belittled, and invalidated your thoughts, feelings, and behaviors, ultimately shaping your self-image and sense of identity. They may have labeled you as "too sensitive," "too emotional," or "too needy," effectively eroding your confidence and convincing you that there was something fundamentally flawed about you.

Reclaiming your authentic self involves the arduous process of disentangling these distorted perceptions from your sense of self. It requires you to actively challenge the negative narratives the narcissist has planted in your mind and replace them with a more objective, compassionate understanding of who you truly are.

Start by carefully examining how the narcissist's criticisms and judgments have influenced your self-perception. Make a conscious effort to identify the specific beliefs, thoughts, and behaviors that have been shaped by the narcissist's distorted lens. Ask yourself: "Is this really true about me, or is this simply a reflection of the narcissist's insecurities and biases?"

As you uncover these distorted perceptions, work to actively challenge and reframe them. Remind yourself that the narcissist's assessments were inherently flawed, born out of their own need for control, validation, and superiority. Their warped perspective does not define your worth or your inherent value as a human being.

One of the biggest impediments to getting back to your true self after narcissistic abuse is having to let go of the narcissist's opinions and their distorted thinking about who you are. The narcissist most likely has transferred his insecurities, bias, and fantabulous sense of reality onto you, resulting in your self-image becoming unclear.

In the course of an abusive relationship, a narcissist may have downgraded, ridiculed, and negated your thoughts, feelings, and behaviors, which in the end, is responsible for shaping your self-image and self-identity. They labeled you as "too sensitive", "too emotional", or "too needy" which harmed your confidence and made you believe that you were inherently flawed.

The multidimensional process of rediscovering the genuine you involves the excruciating work of disentangling these distorted notions from your self-awareness. You are forced to confront the negative script the narcissist has written in your head by replacing it with a more objective, empathetic perspective of who you are in fact.

First, let's analyze how the narcissist's criticisms and judgments have affected your perception and self-esteem. Endeavor to discern the precise beliefs, thoughts, and habits that have been molded by the narcissist's vision twisted from the truth. Ask yourself: "How authentic is this about me, and is it simply a reflection of the narcissist's insecurities and biases?"

As you unpack these misperceptions, work towards actively combating and reimagining them. At the same time, realize that the narcissist's judgments come from their intrinsic flaws, originating from their need for control, validation, and superiority over others. Their misconception of your place in this universe does not devalue your worth or your intrinsic value as a human being.

Redefining Your Identity Beyond the Narcissistic Relationship

While you go through the process of building self-compassion and rediscovering your true self, it becomes very important that you redefine who you are and how you see yourself, looking past the limitations set by narcissistic relationships. The person with narcissism might have tried to make your individuality disappear or changed your life and decisions so they work for their requirements and plan.

After the abuse, it's usual to feel lost and confused about your own identity. You might have trouble remembering who you were before the influence of narcissism took over or find a constant feeling of emptiness or brokenness within yourself.

Getting back your identity includes the act of reconstructing and redefining yourself, removing the control and distortion of character caused by a narcissist. It is necessary to delve into those main elements that make up who you are: your personality traits, values you hold dear, and ambitions that have been suppressed or made unclear by this individual's actions.

Commence with a list of all the roles and identities you have taken on in your life. These might include being a partner, parent, friend to someone, professional worker, or hobby enthusiast among others. Look into which of these parts were genuine reflections of who you are and what was formed by narcissists' expectations or requests.

After finding out the genuine parts of your identity, make a point to grow and encourage them. Get involved in things that match your main beliefs, giving you satisfaction and direction. Fill your surroundings with people who value and help develop the special parts of yourself.

Reformulating identity is not always a clear or linear path. You may experience moments of doubt, unsureness, and even test phases as you steer through this route toward self-realization. Appreciate the changing nature of your character, and let it adapt and modify along with your healing process and personal development.

In addition, pay attention to how the narcissist's effects might still stay with you even if you are trying hard to regain your real self. Quite often, people who have survived narcissistic mistreatment find it difficult to deal with ongoing feelings of doubt about themselves, feeling like an imposter, or having a remaining sense of being "broken" or "inferior."

To oppose these inner stories, you need to be strongly committed to showing self-kindness, accepting yourself, and ready to question the wrong views of narcissism. Appreciate any advancement you make, even if it seems insignificant, and recall that redefining your identity is a continuous life-long journey.

In the end, it is about developing a self-identity that does not depend on the narcissist's confirmation but instead, comes from your values, beliefs, and dreams. While you keep recovering your genuine self, you will discover that real satisfaction and liberty are found in accepting yourself as an exceptional and irreplaceable person.

Chapter 10: Navigating the Grieving Process and Finding Closure

Understanding the Stages of Grief and Loss

The process of healing from narcissistic abuse can be described as a journey through loss - the loss of an imagined perfect relationship, the loss of who you believed the narcissist to be, and finally, the loss of life that was once planned together with them. This grieving stage is often intense, and confusing and sometimes it feels like everything in your world has been taken away.

Understand that the process of grieving you are going through is a normal, required reaction to the hurt and emotional harm caused by the narcissist. Similar to how grief, when someone you love dies, has a clear path it follows, so does grief from losing a relationship because of narcissistic abuse unfold in stages.

The model of the grief process that is known by most people was made by Elisabeth Kübler-Ross and she found five main stages: denial, anger, bargaining, depression, and acceptance. Although these steps might not be in a straight line all the time and can overlap with one another, knowing about every stage's dynamics could help you figure out more about yourself as well as give direction while dealing with your path through sorrow and restoration.

Denial: In the first stage of denial, you might have difficulty accepting that the narcissist is genuinely like this and has caused severe harm to your relationship. This protective reaction lets your mind gradually understand what has happened by reducing or completely ignoring how much abuse has taken place.

Anger: After the denial stage, a powerful surge of anger and bitterness frequently emerges. You might feel extremely furious with the narcissist for their disloyalty, heartlessness, and unwillingness to acknowledge blame in their behaviors. This rage could also be turned towards oneself as you struggle with emotions of self-blame or guilt for not identifying warning signs earlier on.

Bargaining: In this stage, the mind might make a frantic attempt to regain power or undo the loss. You could be thinking about what you did wrong and how things could have been different. The idea of trying to fix the narcissist or get back that idealized image from before might cross your mind as well.

Depression: When you truly understand the loss that has occurred, it can result in a strong feeling of sadness and hopelessness. This could show up as a deep, all-encompassing sorrow marked by emotions of a void, lack of hope, or purposefulness in life.

Acceptance: The last part of the sorrowing process is acceptance - it isn't always about being happy or delighted, but more a place where there's calmness inside and comprehension. This marks when you can start releasing your connection to narcissists' idealized image as well as your connection with them in general, thinking about the future without their sway over you.

Remember that the path of grief is not straight; you might go through these stages several times or in a different sequence. The crucial thing is to display patience, empathy, and kindness towards yourself while handling these intricate emotional territories.

Acknowledging the Need to Grieve the Relationship

A key thing to comprehend in the process of healing from narcissistic abuse is recognizing the deep loss felt and accepting that grieving for this connection is necessary. This can be tough because manipulation and gaslighting from a narcissist might make individuals doubt their feelings or experiences.

Recognize that the sorrow you feel is real and needed for your recovery. The connection you had with the narcissist, even if it was very imperfect and abusive, was a large investment of your time, effort, and emotional strength. So losing this relationship along with an idealized view of them is also a significant loss that needs to be respected and handled with care.

Start by accepting your emotions, not judging or criticizing yourself. Understand that the feelings of loss, sadness, and maybe even betrayal are a normal reaction to the emotional hurt you have experienced. Confirm your own experience, don't reduce or ignore it.

Keep in mind that the grieving process can be complex due to the narcissist's ongoing presence in your life, such as through continuous contact, shared kids, or other involvements. This might make it harder for you to let go and proceed ahead. It could lead you into a cycle of going through grief stages more than once.

In these instances, it's important to put your emotional and physical safety first. You could ask for assistance from trusted allies, therapists, or domestic violence advocates who will aid you in handling the complicated stages of mourning. Keep in mind that your well-being and ability to heal are most important.

As you go through the different phases of grief, show patience and kindness towards yourself. Understand that there is no "correct" or "incorrect" method to grief, and the duration it takes for your recovery belongs completely to you. Have faith that by giving importance to your emotions and dealing with them, you are making an important move towards gaining back control over your life and identity.

Confronting and Releasing the Anger and Resentment

Anger is a very strong emotion that can cause you to feel furious and resentful towards the narcissist. This type of rage, usually hidden below the surface, can be seen as a normal reaction considering the deep violation, betrayal, and emotional destruction you have endured.

Remember, this anger does not depict weakness or immaturity. Instead, it demonstrates your natural understanding of what is fair and how much you long for the narcissist to accept responsibility for their actions. Permitting yourself to experience and show this anger may be a significant part of the healing journey.

However, you must guide this anger towards a beneficial and positive direction. If not managed properly, it can either engulf you or cause more harm to yourself. Anger that is not resolved might appear in various harmful forms such as physical health problems or detrimentally poisonous relationships--leading even to revengeful actions.

Start by making a safe and personal area where you can confront your anger. For example, write a very harsh letter to the narcissist (but don't send it), do intense physical activity, or talk with a therapist for help in handling emotions.

When expressing your anger, remember to recognize if there are any other emotions like pain, disappointment, or sadness hidden within. Accepting the full extent of your hurt might assist in progressing from the initial phase of anger towards comprehension and self-kindness.

It's important to understand that sometimes, the anger may be turned inward. You could feel mad at yourself for not seeing the signals earlier or for thinking it was your fault and carrying guilt around with you. In these moments, step back and repeat to yourself that only narcissists are responsible for abuse – you are the victim not the doer of crime.

Keep on processing and freeing the anger, it might change into a strong motivation for you. The feeling of righteous anger can push you to take back control over your life, establish clear limits, and prevent the narcissist from ever again lowering your value or dictating how things should be.

Acknowledging and valuing your anger instead of pushing it away or rejecting it is an important part of the process of healing and regaining yourself. By directly facing this feeling, you will create a path towards more profound closure, calmness, and strength.

Letting Go of the Idealized Version of the Narcissist

One of the hardest and the most intriguing parts of the grieving process after narcissistic abuse is the necessity to let go of the idealized version of the narcissist whom you loved before. Throughout the relationship, the narcissist may have deliberately groomed a facade of false charm, charisma, and emotional intimacy that made you think that he was an ideal companion, friend, or family member.

Nevertheless, the moment of truth has revealed the real picture, and you now have to grapple with the issue of grieving the loss of the idealized image that you have had of this person – the person you thought they were, and the life you thought you would have lived with them. This might be one of the most painful and disconcerting procedures that you have to undergo, as the narcissist was incapable of true love, empathy, and true inexhaustible emotional investment ever.

First of all, identify the level to which you have been attached to the toxic narcissistic version. Realize that this attachment was not only an innocent show of love, but an intricate scheme that was carefully designed to keep you emotionally attached to the narcissist's plans. The narcissist developed these manipulation strategies, like introducing love-bombing and intermittent reinforcement, to cultivate and preserve this idealized image of you and thereby keep you under their power.

Shedding this deception requires time and compassion for yourself. Narcissist power is probably entrenched in your soul, and it will take efforts and time to undo the hold they used to have on perceptions and emotions.

One useful exercise that can help have the process is to make a list of the real behaviors of the narcissist and their characteristics, rather than the idealized picture you used to dream of. Use this list as a reminder every time you find yourself romanticizing or trivializing the facts about the narcissist's behavior. Tell yourself that you were deceived by a mask that the other person created, not just who the other person is.

Likewise, think about doing some symbolic rituals or activities that symbolize the act of letting go. This could be in the form of writing a letter to the narcissist, which is then burnt or buried, or drawing a picture of the perfect image that was later shattered. Such kinds of rituals offer a concrete and liberating desire to recognize and divest the whole narcissist from your mind and heart.

Ultimately, the process of letting go of your idealized version of the narcissistic person is about getting back your image of reality, the truth, and self-confidence. It's acknowledging that the narcissist's fake image never represented your true worth but served the purpose of exploitation and domination. Through the arduous but necessary process of grief and detachment, you will create a path for yourself to discover a true, authentic self, and your ability to love, connect, and feel fulfilled.

Finding Closure and Acceptance Through Ritual or Dialogue

Part of the challenging and transformative process of moving on from an abusive relationship with a narcissist is to intentionally seek out closure and acceptance. These approaches can vary from participating in symbolic rituals or actively having dialogs with the narcissist, and the conclusion would be to attain a state of peace where you can move on in a new direction.

Many narcissistic abuse victims have continued pain and frustration from not getting any closure or accountability from the narcissists. The narcissist's failure to step up and take responsibility for their actions can in the end just leave you feeling lost, unable to heal properly and whole.

Participating in ritual-based activities may help you attain the empowerment you need to deal with the closure you never got. This could include composing a letter to the narcissist which you afterward burn or bury, thus, the physical act of destroying it represents your emotional release from their approval or validation. Or, you may decide to assemble a visual portrayal of the relationship or the narcissist's negative actions, which you can then ritualistically tear apart or destroy.

Such symbolic acts can be very cathartic because they allow you to release the pain and anger that you held on to. They reinforce the belief that the healing process is in your hands, even if the narcissist does not cooperate.

Sometimes, you may find yourself also adopting a more direct approach that will include talking with the narcissist. This can be done in person or through sending them a statement where you will explain how devastating they have been to you and will demand them to answer for their deeds. Although this course may be difficult and dangerous, depending on the narcissist's temper, it will make you feel liberated and strong eventually.

Being mindful that the narcissist may react with manipulation, denial, or even aggression, it's imperative not to forget about your safety and well-being while doing so.

Consider the involvement of a psychotherapist, domestic violence advocate, or a person whom you can trust and whom you can count on as a reliable source of emotional support for such risks as well.

Finally, the search for closure and its acceptance is a very personal process, and there is no one "right" way to do it. The most important thing is to listen to your intuition, acknowledge the greatness of your emotional self, and search for the tools that will feel the most powerful and connected to your healing process.

While you go through this, know that the real closure and acceptance you are looking for lies not in the narcissist's validation or remorse, but in your strong faith in your intrinsic value and personal capacity to own your life even without that person. Each step you make towards this more authentic and comprehensive peace will place you one step closer to a future that is full of freedom, truth, and the hope of a beautiful life.

Moving Forward with a Sense of Peace and Resilience

At the last stage of the grieving process when you are becoming detached and finding your way toward closure, you may end up standing at the edge of a new and life-changing chapter. The process you went through wasn't an easy one, nor was it a painless one, but by being resilient, brave, and holding fast to the healing of yourself, you found true inner peace after the trauma of narcissistic abuse.

This peace is not just the lack of chaos but knowing that you are valuable, strong, and the real source of determination in your own life. It is the understanding that you have already battled with the deepest shadows inside yourself and the world, and come out on the other side with a higher level of lucidity, a more meaningful purpose in life, and unwavering belief in your right to live a life that is in line with your most true values and ambitions.

As you are approaching this new chapter of your life, you should understand that the path of healing is forever and that this process sometimes will rise and fall with your dynamics. There will be occasions when you return to the stages of grief or when you cannot help but hear the inner voice of the narcissist. To no one's surprise, this will be the case. This, over time, will build up in you the required self-compassion, resilience, and faith in your inner wisdom.

As you embark on this new phase of your life, the important thing is to do so with a mindset of openness, curiosity, and the acceptance that the intricacies and richness of your own lived experiences will be ever-present. Celebrate the achievements you've made, be proud of the scars you bear, and believe that each step taken will get you closer to the life you deserve – the one that is real, fulfilling, and that allows you to be your truest and most inspiring.

As you move along, know that you are never alone. The network of survivors who preceded your way is always there to help you out by sharing the wisdom and experience that they have gained running the same race. Lean on these sources, people, and also professionals, as you are continuously building the resilience, self-compassion, and self-determination that will accompany you through the obstacles still ahead.

In the end, the road to recovery and reclaiming one's self after narcissistic abuse is not about achieving some mythical endpoint, but instead about cherishing and valuing the process itself. It is about discovering joy, meaning, and a deep sense of purpose amid adversities, and about developing indefatigable determination that you and solely you are the writer of your extraordinary life.

And, as you stand on the threshold, take a look back to honor the immense progress you have made, enjoy the inner peace that you have won, and, in the future, set your sights with renewed hope, excitement, and new possibilities ahead of you. You wield the power to forge your future, and the road ahead of you shines brighter and more wonderous than you may presently conceive.

Part IV: Thriving in the Aftermath

In this last part of your trip, pause and think about the amazing progress you have achieved. The road was lengthy, tough, and sometimes appeared too much to conquer. But with your persistent strength, unyielding determination, and strong commitment towards personal healing - you now rise from within narcissistic abuse with fresh power of self-assurance, understanding, and control.

You have gone through many sections where you explored the complicated elements of narcissistic abuse. You discovered how the narcissist used sneaky methods and manipulation tactics to chip away at your self-esteem, as well as keep control over all aspects of your life. You carefully untangled the confusing details about gaslighting and emotional destruction, dealt with lasting trauma connections, and repossessed a genuine identity that is not affected by distortions from narcissists.

Now, at the edge of this last part of your journey, it is time for you to concentrate on the realm of flourishing – taking back your life, constructing a new future, and accepting exceptional freedom and possibilities that are ready for you.

In the upcoming chapters, you will delve into the tactics and instruments needed to surmount narcissistic abuse's consequences. Moreover, they furnish you with wisdom on how to thrive and fabricate a life that matches your core beliefs, ardors, and ambitions. You will acquire skills for handling intricate grief stages as well as finding deep closure which aids in moving ahead with fresh purposefulness and robustness.

Also, you will know how to identify the initial signs of narcissistic behavior. This is necessary because it helps safeguard you from getting involved again and makes sure that what you learned during your journey stays with you in your life ahead.

At last, you will explore the process of transforming your life after being under the control of a narcissist - forming valuable connections, finding satisfying work and interests, and accepting the limitless ability that exists within yourself. This chapter is where you completely recover your freedom, happiness, and strong trust in your infinite capability for development, strength, and self-realization.

In this final part of your journey, you are not alone. You walk with a community of survivors who have already passed through these changes. Each one is proof of the world of unbeatable human strength and ability for healing and transformation. Rely on their knowledge, help, and shared experiences while you keep on writing the next part of your amazing life story.

Now is your time to welcome the freedom, strength, and limitless chances that are there for you. So take a big breath, call up your bravery, and get ready for the next part of your path – a life after a narcissist's touch. It will be full of meaning, satisfaction, and solid belief that you have been all along and still are in charge of shaping your fate.

Chapter 11: Recognizing Red Flags and Safeguarding Your Future

Introduction: Reclaiming Your Power in Relationships

During this hard process of recovery, you may have realized that you have gained really important experience and a new perspective on the matter. Nevertheless, the path to full liberation is still ahead. As a way of protecting your future and regaining your power, be a discerning person and be on the lookout for the red flags and toxic patterns in new relationships so that they don't gain ground and become the trap of your life.

In this crucial chapter, we will explore the main skills and mindset changes that will help you not be surprised by narcissistic exploitation in the future. Through the development of a keener eye for the difference between healthy relationships and toxic ones, defining your limits, and listening to the intuitive voice that is inside you, you will give yourself the power to take a stand and choose those things that boost your self-esteem.

Rewriting your future is not just about not being harmed anymore, it's about having a picture of relationships that are founded based on mutual respect, authentic connection, and unshakable belief that you are worthy of being happy, of having the feeling of being seen, heard and valued for who you are. It is through the knowledge you've acquired and the strengths you've built that you now have the power to make a life filled with sustaining relationships and the deep sense of belonging you were cruelly deprived of.

Hence, let's plunge into this crucial self-protection and self-empowerment process with clarity, bravery, and hearty belief that you create the future you deserve.

Recognizing the Red Flags of Narcissistic Traits

As a result of your turbulent encounter with a narcissist, you may start to be extremely vigilant and careful of any warning sign or emotion that could indicate the presence of the other poisonous individual in your life. This high sensitivity is a natural and normal reaction: your soul has been deeply marred by narcissistic abuse, and your self-preservation mechanism is on alert searching for even the slightest warning signs.

Nevertheless, you need to find a good balance between these two aspects by being careful but not too cautious to the point of projecting your past hurt on everyone in your life. The aim is not to turn into a cynical or paranoid individual, but rather to foster a critical mindset that permits you to glide through the journey of establishing new relationships, with mature judgment, wisdom, and assured self-worth.

The cornerstone is the comprehension of the vital signs and characteristics of the narcissistic personality of an individual. This awareness equips you with a set of red flags to use in detecting potential narcissistic personalities before they can do you the harm of manipulating and controlling you.

Some of the primary red flags to watch for include:

Grandiose Sense of Self and Entitlement: Beware of individuals who exhibit an inflated sense of self-importance, a deep-seated belief in their superiority, and a conviction that they are entitled to special treatment, privileges, and unquestioning admiration. These grandiose tendencies are a telltale sign of the narcissist's fragile ego and their desperate need to maintain the illusion of perfection.

Lack of Empathy and Disregard for Others: Genuine empathy, the ability to attune to and validate the emotions of others, is conspicuously absent in the narcissist. Instead, you may observe a striking indifference to the needs, feelings, and perspectives of those around them, as well as a propensity for exploiting and devaluing their loved ones to serve their interests.

Obsession with Status, Power, and Control: Narcissists are driven by an insatiable hunger for status, power, and control - both over their external environment and the people in their lives. They may exhibit a relentless pursuit of prestigious positions, material wealth, or social validation, all in service of their grandiose self-image and their need to feel superior to others.

Manipulative and Exploitative Tendencies: Narcissists are master manipulators, adept at using a vast array of tactics - from charm and flattery to emotional blackmail and outright lies - to achieve their desired outcomes. They have a remarkable capacity for exploiting the vulnerabilities of others for their gain, often with a complete disregard for the harm they inflict.

Fragile Ego and Inability to Accept Criticism: At the heart of the narcissist's persona lies a profoundly fragile ego, one that is easily threatened by any perceived criticism, failure, or challenge to their self-proclaimed perfection. Their response to such perceived slights is often one of rage, retaliation, and a relentless effort to discredit and devalue the source of the perceived threat.

As you navigate the process of rebuilding your life after narcissistic abuse, be vigilant in scanning for these red flags in any new relationships that begin to take root. Pay close attention to the early warning signs, trust your instincts, and be willing to walk away from any dynamic that appears to mirror the toxic patterns of your past.

Remember, your well-being and your right to be treated with dignity, respect, and authentic care are non-negotiable. By developing a keen eye for these narcissistic traits, you empower yourself to make discerning choices that safeguard your future and pave the way for the fulfilling, nurturing connections you so richly deserve.

Developing a Discerning Eye for Healthy Dynamics

While recognizing the red flags of narcissism is a crucial first step, it is equally important to cultivate a deep understanding of what constitutes a healthy, mutually beneficial relationship. By familiarizing yourself with the hallmarks of positive, supportive dynamics, you'll be better equipped to differentiate between the toxic patterns you've endured and the nourishing connections that will truly enrich your life.

At the heart of a healthy relationship lies a foundation of mutual respect, trust, and emotional attunement. In contrast to the narcissist's self-serving agenda, genuine partners seek to uplift, validate, and empower one another, fostering an environment where both individuals feel seen, heard, and accepted for who they are.

Some of the key characteristics of a healthy relationship dynamic include:

Emotional Availability and Responsiveness: Healthy partners are emotionally available, attuned to each other's needs, and responsive in their interactions. They make a conscious effort to actively listen, validate emotions, and provide empathetic support, creating a safe space for open and honest communication.

Shared Vulnerability and Authenticity: In a healthy relationship, both individuals feel safe to be vulnerable, to share their authentic selves, and to express their thoughts, feelings, and needs without fear of judgment or retaliation. There is a deep sense of trust and a willingness to be seen in one's entirety.

Mutual Respect and Boundaries: Healthy partners respect each other's boundaries, autonomy, and personal space. They engage in open dialogue to align expectations, establish clear limits, and ensure that the relationship remains balanced and free from encroachment or control.

Equitable Power Dynamics: Healthy relationships are marked by a sense of equitable power, where neither partner seeks to dominate or subordinate the other. Decision-making is collaborative, and both individuals have an equal say in the direction of the relationship and the pursuit of shared goals.

Unconditional Acceptance: In a healthy dynamic, partners accept and love each other unconditionally, recognizing and celebrating the other's inherent worth, regardless of their flaws or shortcomings. There is a profound appreciation for each individual's unique qualities and a commitment to supporting their growth and fulfillment.

As you venture forth into new relationships, be mindful of these hallmarks of healthy connection. Pay attention to how you feel in the presence of a potential partner - do you feel seen, heard, and valued? Do you sense a genuine reciprocity of care and respect? Trust your intuition, and be willing to walk away from any dynamic that falls short of the nourishing, empowering bond you deserve.

Remember, the lessons you've learned through your journey of healing have equipped you with an invaluable superpower: the ability to discern toxic patterns and recognize the relationships that will truly enrich your life. Embrace this hard-won wisdom, and let it guide you toward the fulfilling connections that will support your continued growth and liberation.

Setting Clear Boundaries and Dealbreakers

As you navigate the often treacherous landscape of new relationships, one of the most powerful tools at your disposal is the ability to set clear boundaries and establish non-negotiable dealbreakers. These strategies will not only serve to safeguard your well-being, but they will also empower you to take a proactive stance in shaping the dynamics that you are willing to engage in.

Boundaries, in the context of healthy relationships, are the invisible yet inviolable lines that define the limits of what you are willing to accept, both physically and emotionally. They are the uncompromising standards you have set for yourself, the unwavering declarations of what you will and will not tolerate from others.

When it comes to safeguarding your future, you must take the time to deeply reflect on and articulate your boundaries. These may include:

- Physical boundaries: Defining the levels of physical touch, intimacy, and personal space that you are comfortable with.

- Emotional boundaries: Establishing the parameters for emotional vulnerability, honesty, and the respectful handling of your feelings.

- Behavioral boundaries: Outlining the types of conduct, communication, and decision-making processes that you will or will not accept.

- Relational boundaries: Clarifying the level of commitment, exclusivity, and investment you require in a partnership.

Once you have clearly defined these boundaries, you must communicate them openly and unequivocally to any new partner or potential romantic interest. This empowers you to take a proactive stance in setting the tone for the relationship, and it also serves as an early litmus test for the other person's willingness to respect your needs and honor your autonomy.

Alongside these personal boundaries, it is equally important to establish a set of non-negotiable dealbreakers - those red lines that, if crossed, would immediately signal the need to disengage from the relationship, with no exceptions. These might include:

- Any form of physical, emotional, or sexual abuse or violation of your boundaries

- Patterns of dishonesty, manipulation, or a blatant disregard for your well-being

- Attempts to isolate you from your support systems or limit your independence

- Substance abuse issues that compromise the other person's ability to be a healthy, present partner

- An unwillingness to engage in open, honest communication and compromise

By clearly defining these dealbreakers and standing firm in your convictions, you empower yourself to make swift, unapologetic decisions about who you allow into your life, and to remove yourself from any dynamic that threatens to compromise your safety, your self-worth, or your vision for the future.

Remember, your boundaries and dealbreakers are not mere suggestions or vague guidelines - they are the unwavering pillars upon which you will build the healthy, nourishing relationships that you deserve. Embrace them with confidence, and trust that anyone who truly values you will respect and honor the lines you have drawn in the sand.

Trusting Your Inner Voice and Instincts

As you venture forth into the landscape of new relationships, one of your most powerful and reliable allies will be the intuitive wisdom of your inner voice. This innate, gut-level sense of discernment, honed through the crucible of your past experiences, is a priceless tool in your arsenal for identifying potential threats and safeguarding your future.

The narcissist's manipulation tactics were designed to systematically erode your self-trust, to make you doubt the validity of your perceptions and feelings. But through the arduous process of healing and reclaiming your power, you have regained the ability to listen to that inner voice with clarity and conviction.

When it comes to evaluating new potential partners, pay close attention to the subtle signals your body and your intuition are sending you. Do you feel a nagging sense of unease, even if the other person's outward behavior seems perfectly charming and benign? Are there moments where something just doesn't "feel right," even if you can't immediately pinpoint the reason?

Trust those instinctual nudges. They are the product of your subconscious mind, your emotional intelligence, and the hard-won wisdom you've gained through your journey of overcoming narcissistic abuse. Your intuition is a powerful ally, one that can alert you to potential red flags and toxic patterns long before your conscious mind has fully processed the information.

Of course, learning to discern the difference between genuine intuitive wisdom and the lingering echoes of trauma-induced hypervigilance is an important part of this process. You must approach this with self-compassion, acknowledging that your instincts have been shaped by your past experiences, both positive and negative.

One helpful strategy is to take time for quiet reflection, away from the immediate presence of a new potential partner. Tune inward, and ask yourself: "How do I feel when I'm with this person? What is my body telling me, beyond the surface-level impressions?" Pay attention to any visceral sensations of discomfort, anxiety, or a nagging sense of unease. These are often the first signs that your intuition is picking up on something worth heeding.

Additionally, be mindful of any persistent thoughts or gut feelings that seem to linger, even if you can't immediately pinpoint the reason. These may be your inner voice trying to draw your attention to something that requires further examination.

Remember, your intuition is not infallible, and there may be times when it fails to accurately predict a person's true nature. But by learning to listen to it with compassion and discernment, you empower yourself to make more informed choices about the individuals you allow into your life.

Ultimately, trusting your inner voice is an act of self-love and self-preservation. It is a declaration that you value your well-being enough to heed the subtle signals that your subconscious mind is sending you, even when they may be at odds with the outward appearance of a new relationship. Embrace this inner wisdom, and allow it to be your steadfast guide as you navigate the path towards the fulfilling connections you deserve.

Fostering Healthy, Supportive Relationships

As you continue on your journey of reclaiming your life and your autonomy, you must invest in cultivating healthy, supportive relationships that will uplift, empower, and sustain you on the road ahead. These nourishing connections will not only serve as a bulwark against the lingering effects of narcissistic abuse, but they will also provide the fertile ground in which your authentic self can continue to bloom and thrive.

In the aftermath of your trauma, it may feel daunting to open yourself up to new people and relationships. The wounds of betrayal and the lingering echoes of manipulation can make it challenging to truly trust again. However, you must push past this understandable hesitation and make a concerted effort to surround yourself with individuals who will honor your boundaries, validate your experiences, and walk alongside you as you continue to heal and grow.

When it comes to cultivating these healthy, supportive relationships, there are a few key principles to keep in mind:

Prioritize Mutual Trust and Respect: Look for connections where there is a palpable sense of mutual trust, respect, and a genuine commitment to each other's well-being. Avoid relationships marked by power imbalances, control, or the persistent need for validation.

Embrace Open and Honest Communication: Seek out individuals who are willing to engage in open, honest, and vulnerable communication. These are the people who will create a safe space for you to express your thoughts, emotions and needs without fear of judgment or retaliation.

Encourage Empathy and Emotional Attunement: Surround yourself with people who exhibit a genuine capacity for empathy, who can attune to your emotional landscape, and provide the understanding, validation, and support you require.

Foster Equality and Collaborative Dynamics: Gravitate towards relationships where the power dynamics are balanced, where decision-making is collaborative, and where your autonomy and independence are respected and celebrated.

Cultivate Unconditional Acceptance: Seek out connections where you feel seen, heard, and accepted for the fullness of who you are, without the need to perform or conform to someone else's idealized vision of you.

As you navigate this process of rebuilding your support network, be mindful of the pace and flow that feels most comfortable and nourishing for you. There is no need to rush into deep, intimate bonds if your heart and spirit are not yet ready. Instead, focus on cultivating a diverse tapestry of connections - from casual friendships to more profound, mutually supportive relationships - that will collectively uplift and sustain you.

Remember, the individuals you choose to surround yourself with during this pivotal time will have a profound impact on the trajectory of your healing and your future. Be discerning, but also approach this process with an open heart, allowing yourself to be receptive to the possibility of finding true kinship and belonging.

Through the careful cultivation of these healthy, supportive relationships, you will not only fortify your resilience, but you will also create a sturdy foundation upon which to build the life you deserve - one that is rich with the profound fulfillment that comes from being truly seen, heard, and valued.

Prioritizing Self-Care and Emotional Boundaries

As you continue your journey of reclaiming your life and safeguarding your future, one of the most vital and empowering steps you can take is to make a steadfast commitment to prioritizing your own self-care and emotional boundaries. This act of radical self-love and self-preservation will not only nourish your well-being in the present moment, but it will also equip you with the fortitude and resilience to navigate any future challenges that may arise.

In the aftermath of narcissistic abuse, it is all too easy to become consumed by the lingering effects of trauma, to pour all of your energy into avoiding the potential pitfalls and dangers that may lie ahead. While this vigilance is understandable and even necessary to a degree, you must balance it with a steadfast commitment to your own self-care and emotional well-being.

Prioritizing self-care is not a selfish act, but rather a profound act of self-preservation and self-empowerment. By investing in your physical, emotional, and mental health, you fortify your inner resources, replenish your reserves of resilience, and equip yourself to navigate the complexities of rebuilding your life with clarity, purpose, and unwavering self-compassion.

Some key elements of a robust self-care regimen may include:

Physical Self-Care: Ensure that you are meeting your basic needs for nutrition, exercise, sleep, and rest. Engage in activities that bring you joy, comfort, and a sense of embodied presence, whether that's through dancing or simply taking a stroll in nature.

Emotional Self-Care: Make space for regular self-reflection, processing your feelings through journaling, therapy, or creative expression. Cultivate practices that nurture your inner calm, such as meditation, breathwork, or immersing yourself in uplifting music or art.

Mental Self-Care: Challenge yourself intellectually through reading, learning new skills, or engaging in thought-provoking conversations. Invest in activities that stimulate your mind and foster a sense of growth and expansion.

Social Self-Care: Prioritize quality time with supportive, nourishing relationships, while also honoring your need for solitude and space to recharge. Surround yourself with individuals who uplift and empower you, rather than those who may inadvertently trigger remnants of your past trauma.

Alongside these self-care practices, it is equally vital that you establish and maintain firm emotional boundaries to safeguard your well-being. This may involve:

Recognizing Your Limits: Be attuned to the moments when you feel emotionally or energetically drained, and give yourself permission to step back, recharge, and replenish your resources before engaging further.

Setting Clear Expectations: Communicate your needs and boundaries to the people in your life, empowering them to support you in ways that are truly helpful and aligned with your well-being.

Saying "No" Without Guilt: Refuse to compromise your self-care in service of others' demands or expectations. Your personal needs and priorities must take precedence, especially in the early stages of your healing journey.

Curating Your Environment: Thoughtfully consider the media, information, and social connections you allow into your life, filtering out anything that may inadvertently trigger unresolved trauma or undermine your sense of safety and well-being.

As you navigate this path of reclaiming your life and your future, remember that self-care and emotional boundaries are not luxuries, but rather essential tools in your arsenal of resilience and self-empowerment. By consistently investing in your well-being, you send a powerful message to yourself and the world – that you are worthy of care, respect, and the freedom to forge your destiny, unencumbered by the shadows of the past.

Through this holistic approach to self-care and boundary-setting, you will not only safeguard your immediate well-being, but you will also cultivate the emotional and psychological resources necessary to weather any future challenges that may arise. In doing so, you will pave the way for a future filled with the profound fulfillment, joy, and authentic connection that you so richly deserve.

Chapter 12: Empowering Yourself to Create a Fulfilling Life

Reclaiming Your Power and Purpose

You have probably come across countless setbacks, relapses, and times when you lost all hope on your long and difficult narcissist abuse recovery path. The pain of the narcissist's cold-hearted lies and mastery has gone really deep, making you question yourself, the reason for living, and your ability to imagine a future that is independent of your sad past.

Through your sufferings and struggles, there was a giant transformation of your character. Besides that, you have also established a sense of inner power and resilience which will become your basis for building a great life.

In this chapter, we will embark on the transformative journey of rethinking your targets, re-finding your passions, and building a new path for a future that is determined by your true plans and goals. The person you were and your identity will no longer be defined by the narrow-mindedness of the narcissist, who tells you who you should be; instead, you embark on a new journey of self-discovery that taps into the untold potential that is deep within you, and from there, you get the power of spirit and confidence to bring it into existence and fill your heart and soul with energy and happiness.

A comprehensive approach that includes personal growth, fostering supportive relationships, and engaging in meaningful endeavors, will allow you to break the chains of the past and step into the fullness of your life. Each stride you make is regaining your power, purpose, and the soul belief that all possibilities you need lie within yourself.

So, let us begin this journey of self-empowerment, fueled by the hard-won wisdom you have gained and the unwavering conviction that you deserve nothing less than a future filled with hope, joy, and the profound fulfillment of your deepest dreams and aspirations.

Redefining Your Life Goals and Priorities

Another significant step in the journey of recovery from narcissistic abuse is self-reflection and re-evaluation of your life goals and objectives. The control and manipulation activities of the narcissist continuously set you apart from yourself, your true emotions and beliefs, and the life you once dreamed about. Now, it is your turn to reclaim your vision and to give expression to the person you have become in this fire of your healing journey.

In addition to the regular writing of a list of things to do or an ambitious plan, this process is primarily aimed at redefining your life's purpose and values. Unlike this, it is a highly personal and transformative process of self-discovery where you remove many layers of social conditioning, trauma, and outer expectations to finally reveal your true core values and essence.

As you embark on this journey, be prepared to ask yourself some poignant and probing questions:

- What brings me a profound sense of purpose and fulfillment?

- What values and principles do I hold most dear, and how do I want to live them out in my daily life?

- What dreams and aspirations have I long suppressed or abandoned, and how can I now breathe life into them?

- In what ways do I want to contribute to the world around me, to leave a positive and lasting impact?

- How can I redefine success and happiness on my terms, rather than by the standards imposed upon me by others?

Through digging deep into these questions in an honest and vulnerable way, you will begin to unravel the real secret to the kind of life you desire to craft - it will be a life that resonates with your truest passions, your most valuable principles, and your unwavering drive towards realizing your full potential and self - actualization.

Recognize the need to redefine your goals, not limiting them to just the professional and material accomplishments, but also including the wholesome activities that may play the purpose of providing life with deeper meaning. These could be developing stronger and more profound connections with people, delving deeper into creative practices, or dedicating your life to such causes and communities that share your values and bring out your missionary zeal.

Recognize that redrawing your life plans and objectives is not a single-time occurrence, but rather a lifelong process of self-evaluation and adjustment. The beauty of this journey is that you will get more and more realigned with yourself as you evolve and grow toward your future, and you must remain flexible and trust the guidance that comes from your inner wisdom to lead you to the most fulfilling path that matches your truest self.

Through this process of transformation, you will begin not only to take back the power to decide your destiny but also to pave the way for a life that will be replete with meaning, purpose, and the greatly satisfying sense of fulfillment that has been so cruelly denied you in the past.

Pursuing Personal Growth and Self-Actualization

When you find a way to move forward after you get yourself free of narcissistic abuse and start to imagine your life beyond that, you can also undertake a long-term mission of self-growth and self-actualization. Such a commitment to the continuous discovery of your true self and the unveiling of the infinite possibilities for your life are not only a powerful antidote for the psychological scars of the past, but it is also an act of self-love and empowerment that will serve as the cornerstone of the fulfilling future you can now start to create.

During this quest is the acknowledgment that you are not just the collection of terrible events you have experienced, or the narrow perceptions of yourself and the world that the narcissist wanted to impose on you. Similarly, you are a dynamic and complex being, constantly changing and in possession of limitless abilities that involve the transformation, growth, and accomplishment of your deepest desires.

Through a multifaceted approach to personal development, you will empower yourself to shed the shackles of the past, reclaim your sense of agency and autonomy, and step into the fullness of the person you are capable of becoming. This journey may encompass a wide range of enriching endeavors, including:

Continued Healing and Trauma Recovery: Amplify your interaction with therapeutic modalities, support groups, and other resources that would be helpful in the continuous healing and the assimilation of the lessons learned from the ordeal.

Intellectual and Cognitive Growth: Test yourself all the time, by education, either formal or informal, which, at the same time, will give you more knowledge, will sharpen your critical thinking skills, and will wake up your intellectual curiosity.

Emotional Intelligence and Self-Awareness: Foster practices that support your emotional self-awareness, empathy, and skills in working on the complex inner landscape with gentleness and care.

Spiritual and Existential Exploration: Engage in reflective practices, such as reading philosophical or spiritual literature, or consider the ultimate questions of meaning, purpose, and your place in the grand scheme of things.

Creative Self-Expression: Tap into the art that lies within you, using whatever medium you prefer whether it is writing, painting, music, or anything else that brings out what is unique to you.

Physical Health and Vitality: Take care of your physical self through movements, nutrition, and the adoption of lifestyles that invigorate your body and soul, allowing you to fully express the vibrancy of your life.

Through this intricate process of personal development and self-discovery, you will experience not only struggles and successes but also occasions of ultimate fulfillment and times of confusion. Yet, through it all, you will be cultivating an invaluable resource: the unconditional faith that you are the architect of your destiny, the alchemist of your evolution, and the creator of a future that is completely yours to achieve.

Furthermore, in the process of your personal development, you will discover that the dividends of your efforts reach beyond your individual development. Through learning the skills, insights, and traits, you will acquire effective tools to cope with the difficulties of relationships, work, and life in general. It is you who will shine as a symbol of resilience, genuine character, and inner strength, an example to those who are still suffering from the consequences of narcissistic abuse, and a living demonstration to them that the road to self-empowerment is worth all the effort.

Follow this process of personal growth and self-actualization with an open heart and fierce determination. However, through this act, you will not only reclaim your powers, but you will also carve a path that clearly illustrates your utmost wishes and your inner core.

Building a Strong Support Network of Trusted Allies

As you continue to navigate the path of healing and self-empowerment in the aftermath of narcissistic abuse, the cultivation of a robust and nourishing support network will be an invaluable asset in your journey. These trusted allies, whether they be friends, family members, or members of your broader community, will serve as both a bulwark against the lingering effects of your trauma and a wellspring of encouragement, validation, and practical support as you strive to create the fulfilling life that you so richly deserve.

The narcissist's relentless campaign to isolate and control you has likely left you feeling deeply mistrustful of others, wary of opening your heart and allowing new connections to take root. This is an understandable response, born of the profound betrayal and emotional devastation you have endured. Yet, you must summon the courage to begin rebuilding those vital support systems, for it is within the embrace of genuine, unconditional human connection that you will find the strength, the resilience, and the unwavering conviction to forge ahead.

As you set out to cultivate this network of trusted allies, keep the following principles in mind:

Discernment and Boundaries: Approach new relationships with a healthy dose of caution, utilizing the discernment skills you have honed to identify individuals who exhibit the hallmarks of emotional maturity, empathy, and a genuine commitment to your well-being. Establish clear boundaries and communicate your needs openly, empowering others to support you in ways that truly nourish your growth and healing.

Authenticity and Vulnerability: When sharing your story and your struggles, do so with a spirit of vulnerability and authenticity. This not only fosters deeper, more meaningful connections, but it also serves as a powerful act of self-acceptance and self-love - a declaration that you are worthy of being seen, heard, and understood in the fullness of your humanity.

Mutual Support and Reciprocity: Strive to cultivate relationships that are marked by a genuine sense of reciprocity, where both parties feel empowered to lean on one another and to contribute to each other's growth and well-being. Avoid dynamics where you find yourself constantly giving without receiving the nourishment and validation you require.

Diversity and Multifaceted Support: Seek out a diverse array of connections, each offering a unique form of support and perspective. This may include mental health professionals, support group communities, creative collaborators, and trusted friends or family members who can provide emotional, practical, and spiritual sustenance.

Ongoing Maintenance and Renewal: Remember that the process of building and maintaining a strong support network is an ongoing endeavor. As your needs and circumstances evolve, be willing to reevaluate your connections, let go of those that no longer serve you, and proactively seek out new avenues of support and community.

Through this intentional cultivation of a robust support network, you will not only fortify your resilience, but you will also create a tapestry of relationships that will uplift, empower, and inspire you on your journey to self-actualization. These trusted allies will serve as a sounding board for your dreams and aspirations, a source of encouragement and accountability, and a steadfast refuge in times of adversity.

Moreover, the very act of opening yourself up to these nurturing connections will serve as a testament to the healing you have undergone and the profound self-worth you have reclaimed. It is a powerful statement of your commitment to your flourishing, and a declaration that you are no longer willing to go it alone, but rather to embrace the transformative potential of genuine human bonds.

So, embark on this journey of rebuilding your support network with an open heart and a deep well of self-compassion. In doing so, you will not only fortify the foundations of your future, but you will also inspire others who have walked a similar path to follow in your footsteps, forging a community of resilience, empowerment, and unwavering belief in the limitless potential that lies within every one of us.

Engaging in Meaningful Work, Hobbies, and Activities

As you continue to navigate the path of healing and self-empowerment in the aftermath of narcissistic abuse, the intentional cultivation of meaningful work, hobbies, and activities will serve as a powerful catalyst for your personal growth, your sense of purpose, and the realization of the fulfilling life you are now poised to create.

The narcissist's relentless efforts to control and undermine you may have left you feeling disconnected from the very activities and pursuits that once brought you a profound sense of joy, meaning, and self-actualization. Now, as you reclaim your autonomy and your right to shape your destiny, it is time to rediscover and reinvest in the endeavors that truly nourish your soul and ignite your deepest passions.

Whether it be through the pursuit of a meaningful career, the exploration of creative hobbies, or the commitment to community service and social impact, engaging in activities that align with your values, your talents, and your authentic aspirations will serve as a wellspring of empowerment, self-discovery, and the profound sense of purpose that has been so cruelly denied you in the past.

As you embark on this journey of reconnecting with meaningful work and activities, consider the following guiding principles:

Align with Your Values and Passions: Reflect deeply on the work, hobbies, and activities that truly resonate with your core values, your unique talents and strengths, and the vision you hold for the life you wish to create. Seek out endeavors that allow you to make a positive impact, express your authentic self, and feel a profound sense of fulfillment.

Embrace a Balanced Approach: While it is important to immerse yourself in activities that bring you joy and a sense of purpose, be mindful to maintain a healthy balance between your various commitments. Ensure that you are allocating sufficient time and energy for self-care, rest, and the nourishment of your relationships.

Start Small and Build Momentum: If you find yourself feeling overwhelmed or uncertain about where to begin, start small by experimenting with new hobbies, volunteering opportunities, or even part-time work that piques your interest. Allow yourself the space to explore and discover, trusting that the path will reveal itself as you take each step forward.

Celebrate Your Successes: As you engage in these meaningful endeavors, be sure to acknowledge and celebrate your achievements, no matter how seemingly small. This positive reinforcement will not only bolster your self-confidence but will also serve as fuel to propel you onward in your journey of self-empowerment and growth.

Remain Open to Evolution and Adaptation: Remember that your passions, interests, and priorities may shift and evolve. Approach this process with a spirit of flexibility and self-compassion, allowing yourself to let go of activities that no longer serve you and to enthusiastically embrace new avenues of exploration and self-expression.

By immersing yourself in work, hobbies, and activities that are truly meaningful and aligned with your authentic self, you will not only experience a profound sense of purpose and fulfillment, but you will also cultivate a powerful antidote to the lingering effects of narcissistic abuse. These endeavors will serve as a wellspring of self-confidence, mastery, and the unwavering conviction that you are the architect of your destiny.

Moreover, the skills, knowledge, and creative expression you develop through these pursuits will serve as valuable tools in your arsenal as you continue to navigate the complexities of relationships, personal growth, and the ongoing process of reclaiming your life. Each accomplishment, each creative breakthrough, and each moment of deep engagement will serve as a testament to your resilience, your adaptability, and your unwavering commitment to living a life that is truly your own.

So, embrace this journey of rediscovering and reinvesting in the work, hobbies, and activities that nourish your soul. For in doing so, you will not only reclaim your power, but you will also forge a future that is a true reflection of your highest aspirations and your most profound essence.

Practicing Self-Care, Mindfulness, and Emotional Regulation

As you continue your journey of empowerment and the creation of a fulfilling life beyond the constraints of narcissistic abuse, one of the most vital and transformative practices you can cultivate is a steadfast commitment to self-care, mindfulness, and the mastery of emotional regulation. These intertwined disciplines will serve as the foundation upon which you build the resilience, inner peace, and profound sense of self-possession that will empower you to navigate the complexities of life with grace, clarity, and an unwavering sense of purpose.

The narcissist's relentless efforts to control, manipulate, and undermine you have likely left deep scars on your psyche, eroding your capacity for self-care, self-compassion, and the ability to maintain a sense of emotional equilibrium in the face of adversity. Yet, it is precisely these skills and practices that will now serve as your most potent weapons in the battle for your liberation and the realization of the life you so richly deserve.

At the heart of this self-care and emotional regulation regimen lies the cultivation of mindfulness – the practice of present-moment awareness and the cultivation of a deep, abiding sense of connection to the rhythms of your inner and outer worlds. Through the practice of mindfulness, you will empower yourself to break free from the relentless cycle of rumination, anxiety, and the debilitating emotional reactivity that may have plagued you in the aftermath of narcissistic abuse.

Mindfulness, when practiced with consistency and compassion, serves as a powerful antidote to the lingering effects of trauma. By training your attention to dwell in the immediate sensations of the present moment, rather than becoming consumed by the torment of the past or the anxieties of the future, you will create the space to respond to life's challenges with clarity, equanimity, and a profound sense of agency.

Moreover, the cultivation of mindfulness will serve as a vital foundation for the cultivation of other transformative self-care practices, such as:

Somatic Awareness and Embodiment: Learning to tune into the physical sensations and energetic currents within your body, and to honor the profound wisdom and restorative power that resides within your physicality.

Breath-Work and Meditation: Engaging in practices that deepen your connection to your breath, quieting the chattering of your mind, and cultivating a profound sense of inner calm and clarity.

Expressive Arts and Journaling: Exploring creative modalities that allow you to process your emotions, give voice to your experiences, and nurture the unfolding of your authentic self.

Ritual and Ceremony: Designing personalized rituals and ceremonies that honor your journey, celebrate your triumphs, and create sacred space for continued healing and growth.

As you weave these self-care practices into the fabric of your daily life, you will begin to notice a profound shift – not only in your emotional well-being but in your entire orientation to the world around you. You will become less reactive, more attuned to the ebb and flow of your inner landscape, and increasingly empowered to make choices that align with your deepest values and aspirations.

Moreover, the cultivation of this self-regulatory capacity will serve as a bulwark against the lingering effects of narcissistic abuse, equipping you with the tools to navigate life's inevitable challenges and setbacks with a newfound sense of resilience, resourcefulness, and the unwavering conviction that you are the master of your emotional destiny.

Remember, the journey of self-care, mindfulness, and emotional regulation is not a one-time event, but rather an ongoing practice that will evolve and deepen as you continue to unfold into the fullness of your authentic self. Approach it with self-compassion, curiosity, and a willingness to experiment and adapt as your needs and circumstances shift over time.

For in embracing this transformative path, you will not only reclaim your power, but you will also forge the foundations of a life that is truly your own – one that is imbued with a profound sense of inner peace, emotional mastery, and the boundless joy that comes from living in alignment with your deepest truths.

Embracing a Future Filled with Hope, Joy, and Authenticity

As you near the conclusion of this empowering journey of reclaiming your life and creating the future you so richly deserve, it is important to pause and reflect on the remarkable transformation that has taken place within you. From the depths of the pain and trauma inflicted by the narcissist's relentless manipulation and control, you have emerged as a beacon of resilience, self-possession, and an unwavering commitment to living an authentic, fulfilling life on your terms.

Through the arduous process of redefining your priorities, pursuing personal growth, cultivating a robust support network, and engaging in meaningful work and activities, you have not only reclaimed your power, but you have also forged the foundations of a future that is a true reflection of your highest aspirations and your most profound essence. No longer are you bound by the narcissist's narrow vision of who you should be; instead, you have embraced the boundless potential that lies within you and have committed to the ongoing journey of self-discovery, self-expression, and the unfolding of your fullest self.

As you stand on the precipice of this new chapter, it is important to bask in the hard-won wisdom and the deep well of self-trust you have cultivated. Recognize that the challenges you have faced, the lessons you have learned, and the resilience you have developed have imbued you with an invaluable superpower – the ability to navigate life's complexities with a clear-eyed discernment, an unwavering moral compass, and the steadfast conviction that you are worthy of the profound joy, purpose, and authentic connection that you so deserve.

In the days, weeks, and years to come, continue to cultivate a future filled with hope, joy, and the unabashed expression of your authentic self. Embrace the knowledge that the path ahead may still hold its fair share of obstacles and setbacks, but that you now possess the tools, the resources, and the indomitable spirit to meet those challenges head-on, emerging stronger, wiser, and more deeply grounded in your power.

Surround yourself with the nourishing connections and supportive communities that will uplift and empower you, and remain ever-vigilant in protecting the boundaries and priorities you have so intentionally set. Trust in the wisdom of your inner voice, the resilience of your spirit, and the boundless potential that lies within you to create a life that is a true reflection of your deepest dreams and most profound aspirations.

As you move forward, remember that the journey of self-empowerment and the creation of a fulfilling life is not a destination, but rather an ongoing process of growth, adaptation, and the celebration of your unfolding. Embrace each step with open-hearted curiosity, self-compassion, and the unwavering conviction that you are the architect of your destiny.

In doing so, you will not only continue to heal and thrive in the aftermath of narcissistic abuse, but you will also inspire others who have walked a similar path to follow in your footsteps, forging a future filled with profound liberation, joy, and authentic self-expression that is the birthright of us all.

Conclusion: Embracing Your New-Found Freedom and Strength

Before you close this most significant and amazing experience, make sure that you stop, look back, and revel in the huge progress you have made. You have come out of the depths of the narcissist's toxic grip stronger, more battle-scarred, and regained the position as the true king or queen of your destiny.

The road you have traveled has been hard, you've had to face many enemies that were on the verge of drowning you. However, from the very beginning, you have shown a great level of persistence, bravery, and a never-giving-up attitude that is just magnificent. Every barrier you have tackled and every sheet of self-doubt you have shed have turned you into a person of unquestionable strength and purity, that's how I know that the human spirit is invincible.

Look back on the road you have traveled and the realizations that have smashed the narcissist's twists and allowed you to see the world and yourself with a new sense of clarity and self-respect. The revelation that you are not the blemish or the underdog the narcissist had been trying to convince you, but rather, just a whole person filled with natural worth and immense potential.

Give praise to the journey you have overcome, the transformations in your beliefs, and the recovery of your true self. No more are you a hostage to their mood swings, manipulative tactics, and unquenchable hunger for power. You have been liberated from the chains of their control, and thus you have freed yourself, your authority, and your proper standing in the world.

Praise yourself for the strength and bravery you have acquired in this agonizing process. Being able to withstand the narcissist's continual attempts to sack your spirit, reduce your self-esteem, and obliterate your autonomy is evidence of the unbreakable power that lies within you. This resilience that you have developed under difficult times will be a loyal companion as you explore your path towards independence and liberty.

With the lessons and insights you have gained in the course of this journey, the future lies ahead as your guide. Know that you are now no longer under the narcissist's skewed view of reality or the self-limiting ideas that he or she wanted to put on you. The world is your oyster; you have the liberty to find your way and craft a life that can be the true manifestation of your inner core, your driving force, and your most cherished dreams.

Give yourself this encouragement to keep going through the journey of healing and self-exploration which is never whole. Along the way, there will be periods of uncertainty, self-doubt, and aches that will need healing as well. Nevertheless, you have everything you need: the tools, the support, and the unfaltering belief in your worth, to overcome the obstacles that lie ahead of you with finesse and bouncing back ability.

Convince yourself that you are now living a life of purpose, contentment, and the extraordinary freedom you restored for yourself. Let the vision that you form of your future – one full of enjoyment, originality, and a profound sense of self-discovery – be the one who leads you ahead. Build a support group of friends who are your allies for life. They will help you get through the difficult times when you are tired, and they will praise you when you achieve your goals.

Now free from the narcissist's efforts to tame, undermine, or limit the scope of your potential, you have the priceless treasure of boundless power lying in front of you. Trust in the wisdom that you have acquired, the resilience that you have generated, and the unquestionable belief in your inborn preciousness. This is your time to rise and to decisively express the validity of your existence, and to design your life as an accurate representation of your ultimate ambitions and goals.

As you take this decisive step into a new chapter, use the last words of this story as your battle cry against the obstacles you have overcome, and the more impressive journey that lies ahead. You are the portrayal of the resilient human nature, a physical version of what it means to be reborn from trauma and self-determination.

Therefore, stay tall and carry your new ray of hope, courage, and self-conviction to light the way for you. The future is your story to write. You determine the plot, the setting, and the characters. From now on, you tell your own story. This is your time to bloom, to be true to yourself, to fantasize about people who have walked this way to do the same.

Let the freedom and strength find a welcome embrace, as they lay the solid groundwork of a life that will prove to be your manifesto of all that you stand for, your self-worth, and your iron-clad certainty that you, and only you, can be the master of your destiny. The narcissist's power is no more and, in its place, there is a picture of a future filled with hope and assurance that will send shivers down your spine.

So, my dear friend, go forth and conquer. Claim your rightful place in the world, and let your story be a shining beacon of hope and inspiration for all those who have endured the darkness of narcissistic abuse. For in your triumph, we all find the courage to rise, to heal, and to reclaim the extraordinary lives that we were born to live.

About the Author

Monday Farouq, a psychologist and Medical Rehabilitation specialist, is very passionate about helping people recover from toxic relationships. He has deep experience in the area of psychology and rehabilitation. His goal with his career is to give people the understanding and strength to recognize narcissistic abuse's harmful patterns so they can break free from it.

With his kind method and great understanding of how people act, Farouq has helped many people in taking back control of their lives from narcissism. He gives beneficial thoughts and useful assistance not only by doing clinical work but also through writing.

Farouq, the writer of "Escaping the Grip of Narcissism: A Guide to Identifying and Healing from Toxic Relationships," gives a detailed tool for readers to understand and handle the intricate issues linked with narcissistic abuse. His professional knowledge combined with his life encounters make this book an important support for people who want to escape from being controlled by manipulation and find their worth again.

Farouq's dedication to assisting people in recovering from the wounds of narcissistic abuse can be seen in his work. He is a reliable source for those looking for comfort and strength as they navigate their path toward healing.